Graeme Davidson brings to his writing his experience as an Anglican priest, clinical psychologist and lecturer, journalist and religion and ethics columnist, and a software developer. He is a New Zealander who has lived and worked in the UK, California and New Zealand. While a student at Oxford, he was instrumental in setting up a shelter for the local homeless. His books include *Split Decision, Stay? Go? Don't Know! Relationship Matters* and *7Q*, a novel about the finding of the hypothetical Q manuscript, which many scholars believe to be the source of material common to Matthew and Luke's Gospels.

ANYONE CAN PRAY

A Guide to Christian Ways of Praying

Graeme Davidson

Originally published in the USA in 1983
by Paulist Press, Ramsey, New Jersey, USA,
as *Anyone Can Pray: A Guide to Methods of Christian Prayer*
by Graeme J. Davidson with Mary MacDonald

First published in Great Britain in 2008

Society for Promoting Christian Knowledge
36 Causton Street
London SW1P 4ST

The author and publisher have made every effort to ensure that the
external website and email addresses included in this book are correct
and up to date at the time of going to press. The author and
publisher are not responsible for the content, quality or continuing
accessibility of the sites.

All Bible quotations are taken from the HOLY BIBLE,
NEW INTERNATIONAL VERSION, copyright © 1973, 1978, 1984
by International Bible Society. Used by permission of Hodder &
Stoughton Ltd, a member of the Hodder Headline Plc Group.

British Library Cataloguing-in-Publication Data
A catalogue record for this book is available from the British Library

ISBN 978–0–281–06031–3

1 3 5 7 9 10 8 6 4 2

Typeset by Graphicraft Ltd, Hong Kong
Printed in Great Britain by Ashford Colour Press

Produced on paper from sustainable forests

Contents

Preface

Recently, I celebrated the main Sunday service at a neighbouring parish. The gospel lesson was about the disciples asking Jesus to teach them to pray and how he responded by giving them the Lord's Prayer. So, I preached on the topic and, afterwards, members of the congregation crowded round wanting to know more, telling me they hadn't heard a sermon on prayer for years. Their complaint wasn't limited to this particular church, but to most parishes they had belonged to or visited.

Even though they were in prayer groups and many said they prayed privately and were keen on prayer, they felt there was little support for them and it was difficult to find sound practical advice on how to pray.

Most of us are shy about sharing our prayer experiences. Good spiritual teachers are hard to find and in such high demand that they are booked up months in advance. The numerous books and pamphlets on the subject are usually collections of other people's prayers. Many are for one denomination or interest group and use theological language and concepts that can be difficult to understand. They may focus on the theory of prayer or be limited to a few specialized methods.

In fact, learning about the richness and diversity of Christian prayer methods can demand arduous study and amassing a small library – which few of us, however keen we are to learn about prayer, have time to do.

As a result, many people do not extend their prayer horizons. My early prayer life was typical. I was brought up to repeat rote prayers, such as the well-known children's prayers and the Lord's Prayer, and to pour out to God what was on my mind, then wait an obligatory few seconds in silence in case God wanted to reply – which he never seemed to do – and finish with a final prayer. My prayers were verbal and the communication with God one-sided. If I didn't have much to say, I felt I'd failed and I spent the rest of the prayer time thinking about other things. It wasn't until I was preparing for ordination that I gained an appreciation of contemplative silence, structured meditation and the Jesus Prayer – other methods of praying that helped in developing a fuller relationship with God.

It was for this reason I decided to rewrite and update *Anyone Can Pray: A Guide to Methods of Christian Prayer* that I originally wrote with the help of researcher Mary MacDonald while I was living in California back in 1983. Like its predecessor, this revised edition of *Anyone Can Pray* is a basic recipe book – an easy-to-read guide to the wide range of prayer methods. It's a practical prayer guide to the major ways of praying in the various Christian traditions – Protestant, Roman Catholic and Eastern Orthodox. Many methods are common among Christians and some are relevant to only a few, including Christian adaptations of Asian techniques. I have included topics like spiritual directors and teaching children to pray, as well as sections on the fundamental questions of why we pray and how to begin to pray so that the book will serve as a comprehensive text for both individuals and groups.

Anyone Can Pray is for anyone of secondary-school age and onward who would like to develop his or her Christian prayer life. It's a useful companion to refer to for guidance and as a stimulus to your prayer life. As the book is practical and expansive in its scope and each topic is short and self-contained, it is easy to digest and use with classes and groups as well as with individuals.

I have deliberately avoided suggesting that any method is better than another. They are merely different. Each of us will prefer a different style of prayer at one point in our lives and another as our prayer life develops.

My own experience of teaching classes on prayer is that many Christians are reluctant to admit they haven't really thought about why they should pray or what they should pray about but are keen to step out of their tradition and learn about unusual meditation and contemplative methods. In spite of the allure of the exotic, I recommend that groups, in particular, start by considering the basic questions relating to their own prayer in their own words. Although there is no progression from so-called elementary to advanced forms of prayer, and although each topic is self-contained, it would be advisable for a group to study the first three sections in sequence before looking at other topics.

By beginning with a discussion on the fundamentals, the group members will be better prepared and more enthusiastic and confident about trying out the methods and sharing their experiences. After all, the best way to learn about prayer is to try it.

I feel certain the procedures outlined in this book will help you to extend your prayer life and to grow in your love and devotion to God.

Graeme Davidson
Havelock North
Hawke's Bay
New Zealand

1
WHY PRAY?

Anyone can pray

Anyone can pray. It's as simple as getting in touch with your best friend. You don't need to be a saint. And you definitely don't have to have a degree in theology, a particular type of personality or special spiritual attributes. People from different age groups and conditions can pray. I've listened to the compelling prayers of a murderer and someone with Down's syndrome, the almost inarticulate utterances of a bed-ridden quadriplegic and the erudite prayers of poets and academics. Jesus selected ordinary people – fishermen, a freedom fighter, and a tax collector – as his disciples, and taught them how to pray. If they could learn, we can, too.

Prayer is as easy as making contact with that best friend who's right there beside you. All you need to do is focus on God and let him reach out to you. It helps if you have the right attitude: humility and a genuine desire to communicate. That's all it takes. From the moment you really want to make contact with God you've already begun to pray.

You might think you haven't a prayer. Maybe you feel embarrassed about how you've treated God or that you're unworthy and he'll want nothing to do with you. Perhaps you think the two of you don't have much in common. God's an alien who exists in a different realm from you and you don't know how to break the ice. Or worse, it'd be a fruitless, negative experience. So, why bother?

Despite your misgivings, God still loves you and wants to hear from you. So don't be shy. You can tell God what you think of him, your faults and how you mess up, what you're thankful for and what you need.

You don't have to say much. There are many ways of praying. You can remain silent in God's presence, voice a simple cry, meditate on the gospel message, reflect on creation, write a letter or chat with God and listen to what he's telling you. As in any dynamic relationship, you need to remain flexible in how you communicate. Be prepared, though, to have your life turned upside down.

God is the best friend you'll ever have. His love for us is such that we can always rely on him to listen to our prayers. His calendar is never so full that he can't fit us in. The psalmist explains it like this, 'The LORD is near to all who call on him, to all who call on him in truth' (Ps. 145.18).

Why pray?

The answer is simple. 'We love because he first loved us' (1 John 4.19). We pray to God because he loves us and because we want to love him. People in love enjoy being close to each other. They want to know how their partner thinks and feels and what they can do to make him or her happy. If I told you how much I love my wife and then added that I hadn't bothered to communicate with her for the last couple of years, or that I only got in touch at a Sunday function or when there's a crisis, you'd doubt my sincerity. Yet I've met plenty of Christians who claim to love God but haven't been in touch for ages, or only when they go to church or when they're desperate. It's as if they've put God on hold while they get on with their lives.

When Jesus commanded us to love God with all our heart, soul and mind (Mark 12.30), he meant that we should commit ourselves wholeheartedly to God. That means you can't love God by proxy through the prayers of others. He loves you. So, he wants to hear from you. You can share all your thoughts, feelings, and experiences – your joys, sorrows, problems, fears, hopes, failures, embarrassments and thoughts – in the full knowledge that God will understand and love you.

Even if you've drifted apart from God or treated him badly he will continue to love you. That's the theme of the Bible. Jesus told many stories to illustrate this, including the well-known parable of the prodigal son. Even though the son took his inheritance, left home and squandered it on a dissolute lifestyle, his father still welcomed him home with great joy (Luke 15.11–32). It's what Jesus' mission was about and why he died for us.

Frequently we cast aside our Lord's first commandment in favour of the second, of loving our neighbour as ourselves (Mark 12.31). Most of us lead busy lives and the needs of those around us appear so pressing that we give them priority over prayer. As society judges us by our good deeds and attitudes towards others rather than the quality of our spiritual lives, we find it easy to neglect prayer.

While it's essential that we care for others, our love and concern should involve more than an act of humanism. It needs to flow from our loving, close relationship with God. If not, we become like the parent who's so preoccupied with work and worthwhile charitable projects that the relationship with the family deteriorates – a common complaint of clergy families. Far from inhibiting our outreach, our active love for others is enhanced by regular prayer. The Albert Schweitzers (1875–1965) and the Mother Teresas (1910–97) of this world were fuelled by prayer. Mother Teresa stressed, 'Everything starts from prayer.' They, along with countless Christians, stress that it has been through prayer that they have been able to accomplish much. A quote attributed to St Augustine of Hippo (354–430) expresses this succinctly: 'He that loveth little, prayeth little; he that loveth much, prayeth much.'

Jesus' own prayer life is an excellent example to follow. He prayed frequently and taught us to pray using the Lord's Prayer. He also made the outstanding assertion: 'If you believe, you will receive whatever you ask for in prayer' (Matt. 21.22). To illustrate what he meant, Jesus claimed that if we had enough faith we could move a mountain and cast it into the sea. Some of us take this saying at face value. We believe that if we muster enough faith, God will always act on our behalf. Is that what Jesus meant? Or was he exaggerating and using a parable to make a point?

While working as a journalist, I reported an airline crash. 'As we started to take off down the runway', one of the survivors recalled, 'I knew we were in serious trouble. So, for the first time since I was a kid, I prayed. I don't mind admitting it. I prayed like mad.' As this man felt powerless, he had turned to prayer as others might turn to thoughts of their loved ones, fill their minds with positive images or trust to a lucky charm. Fear for his life had driven him to clasp at prayer like a drowning person clasps at the proverbial straw.

Some of us treat our prayer life in a similar way. When the things we trust fail, nations go to war, people we love have an incurable illness or we are worried about whether we can pass an exam, we look to God miraculously to bridge the gap – or move the mountain.

In the influential *Fortnightly Review* of 1 August 1872, Francis Galton (1822–1911) caused a stir in Victorian society when he reported one of the earliest experiments on the effectiveness of prayer. Thousands of British people prayed for the monarch every Sunday. So Galton checked on whether the royals lived longer than other groups in the general population. His statistical analysis revealed they didn't.

Had he shown prayer is a waste of time? Or at best, that it only acts as a placebo to boost morale and make us feel good?

Jesus illustrated the effectiveness of prayer by pointing to how God is like a friend who will help a neighbour when a guest visits or a father who will provide for a son who asks for fish or an egg. He asserted that whatever we ask for we will receive (Luke 11.1–13). Galton's approach misunderstands what effective prayer is. God is not there to respond to what we want or to make us feel good. It could even be said that the more we try to put God to the test, the less likely he is to respond.

More experiments have shown prayer to be ineffective than effective. Some recent research even shows that prayer produces negative rather than positive results. That could be because the experimenters often view prayer as a magical formula that produces unexpected and measurable changes.

We, too, can expect God to act like a super-genie that our prayers unleash from a heavenly Aladdin's lamp to provide instant solutions. The reverse is true. Effective prayer isn't about how best to manipulate God to respond to our will, but opening ourselves to the guidance of the Holy Spirit so that we become the instruments of his will. This is what Jesus suggested when he finished his discussion on prayer with the disciples by saying, 'If you then, though you are evil, know how to give good gifts to your children, how much more will your Father in heaven give the Holy Spirit to those who ask him!' (Luke 11.13).

God often uses us to answer our own prayers. With this view in mind, many Christians have opted for a metaphorical interpretation of Jesus' comment about casting a mountain into the sea through prayer. The mountain Jesus refers to would be a figure of speech for some of the seemingly insurmountable problems we face. Jesus implies that if we truly trust God, he will lead us to an answer through the power of prayer. If we really do need to remove a mountain, these days the Holy Spirit is likely to point us in the direction of modern engineering techniques. And, if we pray for the long life of the royal family or anyone else, then we'll need to do what we can to give them a healthy, supportive and secure environment. Similarly, if you are seeking for that right person to spend the rest of your life with, you're not going to find him or her by sitting at home watching romantic films on TV. You're more likely to find each other in the most unlikely of circumstances. My wife and I met at a very boring formal church conference – hardly the ideal romantic setting to set hearts ablaze. But we knew that God had used that setting for us to recognize what we had in common and what each could bring the other.

However Jesus' illustration is understood, prayer can have an enormous impact on the world.

People throughout the ages have made remarkable claims for prayer – from the miraculous healing of incurable illnesses to the conversion of hardened criminals. One elderly woman whom I visited complained about feeling lonely and worthless. She admitted she often felt like committing suicide. Her family lived abroad and she was in constant pain from arthritis and had great difficulty moving about her small apartment. When she told me how depressed and desperate she felt, I reminded her of the first commandment and suggested that she spend time coming to know God better through prayer and study. At first, she was sceptical. She wanted to do something more practical. I had to assure her that if she came to God in prayer, she would experience the joy of his company and love and that this would give purpose to her life. As the weeks passed and she became occupied with her devotions, she started to radiate a sense of inner peace. Neighbours noticed the change. Instead of a tiresome and embittered old woman, she had become welcome company. People enjoyed visiting her. Some even began to re-examine their own faith. Everyone benefited from her prayer life.

God doesn't always give us peace and inner strength when we pray, nor should we expect this. At one point, the psalmist complains of how he derives no comfort from his frantic pleas for help:

> When I was in distress, I sought the Lord;
> at night I stretched out untiring hands
> and my soul refused to be comforted.
>
> I remembered you, O God, and I groaned;
> I mused, and my spirit grew faint.
> (Ps. 77.2–3)

We, too, can lose heart when we don't seem to be receiving instant answers to our prayers. But don't give up; it sometimes takes time. God reveals his answer only when we are ready to receive it. In his play *An Ideal Husband*, Oscar Wilde (1854–1900) quipped, 'When the gods wish to punish us they answer our prayers.' The answer may require more of us than we initially want to give. We need time to adjust our thinking to what God wants.

In the same way in which applicants for a job are often tested to check how worthy they are for the tasks they need to perform, God may challenge and test us. This is a constant theme throughout the Bible – the Israelites during their 40 years in the desert, Job's misfortunes, the temptations Jesus faced during his 40 days in the desert (Mark 1.13) and the challenges of the early Church. Jesus and St Paul urge us to have faith and be persistent in prayer. We need to persevere, not because God is forgetful and needs a constant reminder or because our prayers have a short 'use by' date. Nor is it a question of continuing to pester God until our prayers rise to the top of the pile of his 'to do' list. It's so we can remain continually open to his direction.

We often pray for peace in the world and many of us must despair when yet another outbreak of hostilities occurs. But we should always have hope. It took many years of prayer and perseverance during periods of severe persecution and martyrdom before the early Church was accepted by the Roman Empire. Despite the impression we get watching the news, recent research for the United Nations suggests casualties from armed conflicts have dropped dramatically over recent years. If we persevere in our prayers, God will show us what part we can play to bring about a just peace. He might lead you to raise issues to a politician about your country's foreign policy, or contribute to refugee relief, or join a medical or peacekeeping team. You may feel helpless but never underestimate what God can do through you. Very ordinary people – like Jesus' disciples, Francis of Assisi (1181–1226) and Ignatius of Loyola (1491–1556) – performed extraordinary feats through the power of prayer.

Prayer can help us put our worries and concerns into proper perspective. When we approach God with our problems, we know that he will listen and understand. We can unburden ourselves to him and pour out what's on our mind. Jesus made that clear when he said, 'Come to me, all you who are weary and burdened, and I will give you rest' (Matt. 11.28). Once we share our troubles with God and concentrate on his boundless love, things can start to fall into place.

Be aware, though, that this doesn't always happen. Sometimes the stress levels increase as we wrestle with God and ourselves in prayer. That's because there's a clash of wills between what we want and what God wants, or we don't have faith that what God wants will work. We fear failure.

Most of us don't like it when God says no to our requests or wants us to do the opposite of what we think is best. Jesus was distressed and overwhelmed with sorrow before his arrest in the Garden of Gethsemane. He fell on the ground and reminded his heavenly Father that, as everything was possible with him, he could let him off the hook. 'Yet not what I will, but what you will' (Mark 14.36) was how Jesus ended his prayer. That should be your aim, too. After all, when Jesus was predicting his death, he told us that we would need to take up our cross daily if we follow him (Luke 9.23).

Why should we bother to pray to God, when, as Jesus said, 'Your Father knows what you need before you ask him' (Matt. 6.8)? If God already knows what we need, surely it is presumptuous and redundant to pray to him. Nonetheless, although he knows what we are thinking, that doesn't mean we should neglect prayer. If we never pray, we shut ourselves off from a unique and wonderful loving relationship and a chance to learn his will for us. As the Danish philosopher Søren Kierkegaard (1813–55) wrote in his *Upbuilding Discourses in Various Spirits*: 'Prayer does not change God, but it does change the one who prays.'

What's your excuse?

We can always make excuses for why we haven't prayed. Most of us would like to pray more than we do but somehow we never get around to it. We're too busy dealing with a crisis, too tired, something else crops up, or else we are not in the right mood. Priests and pastors who hear private confessions say that failing to pray is the most frequent admission they hear. Recent surveys show that prayer has slipped to near the bottom of church priority lists, Christians are praying less than they used to several decades ago and clergy seriously neglect their own private devotions. Like the disciples who couldn't stay awake to pray with Jesus, our 'spirit is willing, but the body is weak' (Mark 14.38).

How do we overcome our inertia? It's just a question of getting started. As a child, I did anything to avoid taking a bath. I became adept at inventing elaborate excuses. Yet, once I was immersed and playing in the water, my parents had a hard time getting me out. Often we feel so embarrassed about our lack of prayer that we are incapable of beginning. We feel so hypocritical and uncomfortable approaching God that we snub him. And because we snub him, we feel even more awkward about making contact. The longer we leave it the more self-conscious we become.

There's only one way to break this impasse. Accept that God's not going to scold you for truancy and that he's always delighted to hear from you. Like the prodigal son that Jesus spoke of (Luke 15.11–32), once you've broken the ice and re-established contact, you'll find that God really does love and accept you. Like my childhood experiences with taking a bath, you might find you enjoy the experience and may even be a little more eager next time.

Don't give in to the temptation to leave it to experts to pray to God on your behalf. When we hear the eloquent prayers of others and learn about the lives of people in religious orders who dedicate themselves to prayer, it's natural to feel inadequate – but God loves you and wants to be in a loving relationship with you.

We don't have to have a wall full of framed degree certificates in psychology and communications from prestigious institutions to have wonderful relationships with people. So, why should we expect to be experts on prayer when we pray? Once we sincerely desire to be with God we have begun to pray and he reaches out and responds as any loving partner does – delighted that you've made contact.

Yet, many of us still can't believe that God will accept us. I've heard people tell of how they've lied, cheated, stolen, been unfaithful to their partner, assaulted, abused or taken unfair advantage of others. The people I worked with in prison knew Jesus offered sinners hope and forgiveness, but they had committed so many heinous crimes they were ashamed of, and most assumed it applied to others, not to them.

It seemed to me they punished themselves by pushing God away and denied themselves the opportunity of experiencing his healing love. Perhaps they were too proud to accept his free offer of reconciliation. They needed to be reminded that even the disciples, who knew very well what Jesus expected of them, broke their promises and let him down during his trial and crucifixion; and how Paul of Tarsus persecuted and killed Jesus' followers, believing it to be the will of God – until he had a revelation on the road to Damascus. If God's love could extend to them, surely it can extend to those of us who feel we're unworthy.

Some critics accuse the Church of instilling an unhealthy sense of shame and guilt. They seem to ignore that the whole thrust of our faith is towards God's loving acceptance, no matter what we've done. Far from carrying the burden of destructive emotions like guilt, we should be radiating God's love.

Many critics accuse us of using religion as an emotional crutch. In his 1843 *Critique of Hegel's Philosophy of Right* Karl Marx (1818–83) gave us this well-known quote: 'Religion is the opium of the people.' The implication is that we lean on God to get us through situations that we can't face ourselves. That assumes our faith is a selfish one and that prayer is a way of making us feel euphoric as we try to cope with each day. The opposite is true. Far from recommending an opiate, Jesus challenges us to deny ourselves, take up our cross daily (Luke 9.23) and, through God's grace, strive to be more loving. Jesus used the illustration of a narrow gate and road (Matt. 7.13–14) that is difficult for his followers to find compared to the wide gate and broad road that is the easy path. His own lifestyle was a good example, as are the lives of many saints throughout the ages who've followed him at great personal cost. It certainly wasn't an easy path and many chose to die rather than compromise their faith.

Plenty of romances start with the couple disliking each other intensely. They antagonize each other, spar verbally and may even disparage each other with phrases like, 'He's the last person in the world I'd ever want to date', or, 'Can't imagine why anyone would be attracted to her.' It often takes a while before the couple realize they're fighting an attraction for each other. Perhaps they're frightened of what being in love may involve and how it might change their lives. Maybe they'll get hurt.

Plenty of us fight our attraction to God and his love for us. In the book of Genesis (Gen. 32.22–32) there's an account of Jacob wrestling with a strange man who turns out to be God. It's an odd story, but it illustrates the kind of struggle we can have when we begin to pray. Maybe we don't really want to be in love with God and allow him to change our lives. He'll make too many demands and we'll get hurt.

In his *Confessions*, St Augustine of Hippo (354–430) described his spiritual journey and how in his early life he avoided God by adopting other philosophies and lifestyles, including having a child out of wedlock. Often quoted from the *Confessions* is his prayer, 'Grant me chastity and continence, but not yet.' It shows that even a saint like St Augustine was human and in the beginning wrestled and bargained with God.

In recent times, the Trappist monk and author, Thomas Merton (1915–68), led a similar dissolute lifestyle, which he wrote about in his *The Seven Storey Mountain*. As many saints have done, he found God through struggle and clash of wills – until he was ready to submit to God's love. Even then, he wasn't sure. In his book *Thoughts in Solitude*, he began his most famous prayer with the words:

> My Lord God, I have no idea where I am going.
> I do not see the road ahead of me.
> Nor do I really know myself.
> And the fact that I think I am following your will
> Does not mean that I am actually doing so.

When lovers in romance novels do realize they love each other, the tension falls away and they feel free, happy and at peace. Accept that as you begin to approach God in prayer there's likely to be a struggle and that it's only by persevering that you'll come to that place where, surrendering to his love, you will experience a newfound freedom, inner peace and joy.

Our doubt can act as a major block to prayer. Questions about God's existence, his relationship with us and the value of prayer often interfere. Most of us live in materialistic consumer-driven societies where many people are sceptical of religious practices like prayer. They usually see them as superstitious relics of a bygone age. Over recent years, the views of atheists and disaffected believers have been voiced in popular books and given wide media coverage. Some commentators have even called these disbelievers the 'new evangelists'.

It's hard to pray to God if you believe he's gone into hibernation. Yet, our lack of faith need not be an insurmountable barrier. Jesus understood Thomas' disbelief about the resurrection – and Thomas was one of the disciples! Surely, God will help us with our doubts if we let him know what we're thinking. Unless we ask for help for what's undermining our faith, how can we be open to God's direction? Our doubts can be as much the subject of prayer as any other topic, so don't hesitate to confront God with your misgivings. When Jesus asked the father of the epileptic boy possessed of an evil spirit whether he believed, he replied, 'I do believe; help me overcome my unbelief!' (Mark 9.14–25). You should be as honest with God.

There will probably be stages in your life when you're so riddled with doubts that you'll barely be able to utter a word to God. French philosopher Ernest Renan (1823–92) must have prayed the ultimate doubter's prayer, when he wrote in *Prière d'un Sceptique*:

> O Lord, if there is a Lord,
> Save my soul, if I have a soul.

At least he was still praying. He was being honest with God, and that's what you should be. Don't expect your doubts to disappear overnight. Despite her well-publicized work with the poor and dying and the founding of the Missionaries of Charity, Nobel Peace Prize-winner Mother Teresa of Calcutta (1910–97) suffered feelings of spiritual loneliness and doubts for decades. In an undated letter addressed to Jesus at the suggestion of a spiritual advisor, she wrote:

> I am told God loves me – and yet the reality of darkness & cold-
> ness & emptiness is so great that nothing touches my soul. Did
> I make a mistake in surrendering blindly to the Call of the Sacred
> Heart?   (*Come Be My Light*)

Her experiences are those of the 'dark night of the soul' described by St John of the Cross (1542–91; see *The Mystical Way*).

Like Mother Teresa and St John of the Cross, you'll need to per-severe and follow Jesus' advice to 'always pray and not give up' (Luke 18.1).

At times, we can become furious with God. We blame him for our problems and suffering. When her daughter, born with a defective heart, died prematurely, a woman in my parish in England raged when I visited her, cursing God for taking her daughter. She wasn't in the mood to pray. But why shouldn't we confront God with our anger, especially when we're frustrated by what we think is his lack of love and concern for us?

The psalms are full of complaints and railings at the way God seems remote and inactive. While he was on the cross, Jesus repeated one of these cries of despair: 'My God, my God, why have you forsaken me?' (Ps. 22.1; Mark 15.34). People in love often give vent to their feelings when they're upset. It helps bring those feelings into the open so that issues can be resolved. Similarly, if you share your anger with God, it will help you come to terms with him and his will. It's when you can't be bothered to respond to God at all that the relationship is in danger of collapsing.

It's natural to feel apprehensive about coming before God. He's the Almighty Lord who's beyond our comprehension, yet we're putting our trust in him. We're inviting God to judge, challenge, transform and take charge of us. And that can be a daunting prospect. Perhaps that's why many of us can only take being with God in small doses. We feel he's too overpowering. So, we limit our prayer to the occasional short burst when we're up to coping with him.

The closer we come to God, the more we become aware of the contrast between our shortcomings and his majesty. Because of this gulf and the effect God can have on us as he helps us to bridge the gap, Metropolitan Anthony Bloom (1914–2003) of the Russian Orthodox Church described prayer as a dangerous adventure. He says that we put ourselves at risk whenever we approach God and that we need courage to pray.

Of one thing you can be certain: the encounter will not leave you the same.

2
BEGINNING TO PRAY

Finding the time

It's an excellent ideal to pray when you rise; then you won't have the chance to put prayer off until later in the day when you may feel less inclined.

So, pray when you rise – and before going to bed – in order to begin the day with praise and end with thanksgiving. This helps to open ourselves to God's guidance 24/7.

Praying at set times during the day and even during the night was a common practice in the early Church. Psalm 119.164 says: 'Seven times a day I praise you.' This is probably what Jesus did and those first Christians continued with the Jewish practice of praying at set times throughout the day. Their prayers would have included readings from the Law – the first five books of the Hebrew Bible – and reciting psalms and other Jewish prayers. The earliest Christian manual we have, the *Didache*, written within a century of Jesus' crucifixion, recommends praying the Lord's Prayer three times a day.

As they moved away from their Jewish roots and new believers from throughout the Roman Empire joined the infant Church, many Christians prayed a cycle of prayers in keeping with the way the Romans divided their working day into three-hourly segments. Prime, or first hour, was at 6 a.m. Terce was at 9 a.m., followed by Sext at noon. The lunch break ended with None, or ninth hour, at 3 p.m. and the workday ended at 6 p.m. Over the years these prayer times grew into the monastic practice of praying Mattins during the early hours of the morning, Lauds prior to dawn, Prime at 6 a.m., Terce at 9 a.m., Sext at midday, None at mid-afternoon, Vespers at sunset and Compline to complete the day with bedtime prayer. These daily prayer times can vary but there are usually special prayers, readings and meditations that are standard for each prayer time.

But let's be honest. Most of us would find it very difficult to stick to a monastic-style prayer regime. Even the thought of praying on rising and before bed can be difficult for those of us with young families, long commutes to work and long hours once there. We're too exhausted at bedtime and the best television programmes always seem to be on late. And even though many early Christians did what Jesus advised – that we 'keep watch, because you do not know the day or the hour' (Matt. 25.13) when he would return – very few of us have the fortitude and discipline to wake during the wee small hours to pray. We need to find sensible times when we can give God our full attention.

Although you can pray at any time, it's worth setting aside some fixed prayer periods during the day when you can give God some quality time. Perhaps you could pray after you've showered and dressed, after breakfast, or even while you commute to and from work. In the evening, you might pray after your meal, or before you socialize or settle down to watch television. You could also pray at lunchtime, during a coffee break or while taking the dog for a walk or jogging. Don't forget the shorter forms of prayer that you can use at any spare moment.

Jesus told the parable of the pushy friend (Luke 11.5–10) and the persistent widow to illustrate how we should pray persistently and not give up (Luke 18.1–8). After Jesus' crucifixion, the disciples, along with his mother, brothers and some of his women followers, prayed continually (Acts 1.13–14) and Paul instructed the Thessalonian Christians to 'pray continually' (1 Thess. 5.17).

That seems like a tall order. How can we pray 24/7? The Desert Fathers, who flourished during the third to sixth centuries, lived Spartan lives devoted to prayer in the wilderness areas near Egyptian cities. They became the first Christian monks and some, especially the hermits, spent most of their waking hours in solitary prayer. Others organized their communities into a series of continuous hour-long prayer vigils so that there were always some of them praying at any hour of the day or night, 24/7, 365 days a year. That was their idea of praying without ceasing. How can we possibly do something like that if we have to earn a living, spend time with the family, do shopping and other chores and have some well-earned leisure time?

Paul wasn't expecting us to spend 24 hours a day on our knees. He certainly didn't do it; he spent time travelling, preaching, teaching, writing letters and working as a tentmaker. What he emphasized is that we should aim to make our whole life a prayer, that we should constantly respond to God's presence.

It's similar to what happens when we love someone. We alter our lives to fit in with that person, who becomes the focus of our attention. He or she is like our shadow – always there shaping our thinking, feelings and behaviour.

To follow Paul's advice, you will need to make God the centre of your being so that you become like his shadow. That means being constantly aware that you are in God's company, and letting that experience influence you, so that everything you do, think and feel becomes a prayer.

The Benedictine order, which has inspired monastic thinking in the West for the last 1500 years, adopted the motto *Ora et labora* – pray and work – which embodies this idea. This could become your ideal, but watch you don't substitute work for prayer. There are plenty of Christian activists so busy doing the Lord's work they have little time to spend with God. Try to avoid this trap.

Choosing a place

You can pray anywhere. You don't have to be around other Christians, stained-glass windows or icons. You don't have to stare at a crucifix, sit in a pew or gaze at the beauty of nature. Jesus certainly didn't confine his praying to the temple or synagogues. He prayed in a garden, on a mountaintop, in the desert, by a lake; he prayed before meals, in a lonely or private place, in a 'certain place', at the Last Supper and on the cross.

Throughout history, people have selected some extraordinarily diverse places in which to pray. Simon the Stylite (389–459) was a hermit who spent 37 years in Syria on top of several tall pillars, beginning with one 6 metres high, then 11 metres, before finally graduating to 16 metres near the end of his life. He did this to elevate himself above worldly concerns and temptations to rise closer to God. Thalelaeus of Cilicia (*c.* 450) chose to live in a haunted cemetery near a disused pagan temple in Syria. He endured ten years of solitary penance and prayer living in a cramped hut the size of a barrel. Bishop Kentigern (*c.* 518–603) of Scotland slept on a bed of stone, fasted and prayed naked in the Clyde River, sometimes reciting all 150 psalms in one session. Today we would view this kind of behaviour as masochistic and symptomatic of a psychiatric illness. Yet, these saints were taking seriously Jesus' command to his disciples to deny themselves, take up their cross and follow him (Mark 8.34).

While you don't need to find a place that'll mortify the flesh to this extent, it's a good idea to find a spot that'll help you concentrate on God.

The solitude of the desert has attracted many. Jesus' experience of facing temptations in the desert and John the Baptist's wilderness life in the Judean Desert inspired tens of thousands of Christians during the third to the sixth centuries. These Desert Fathers (and Mothers) lived an austere, ascetic life of prayer near Egyptian towns, especially in the Nitrian Desert at Wadi El Natrun, between Alexandria and Cairo. More recently, the French spiritual writer, Charles de Foucauld (1858–1916), became a hermit in the Algerian Sahara, while the famous rocket pioneer, Wernher von Braun (1912–77), often interrupted his work in his later years in the USA to take long rides into the desert to pray.

A humble Carmelite monk, Brother Lawrence (*c.* 1614–91), worked at menial tasks in the monastery kitchen, where it dawned on him that God is always present and he could pray just as well among the pots and pans: '. . . in the noise and clutter of my kitchen, while several persons are at the same time calling for different things, I possess God in as great tranquillity as if I were upon my knees at the Blessed Sacrament' (*The Practice of the Presence of God*, 4th Conversation). He concluded:

> It is not necessary for being with God to be always at church; we may make an oratory of our heart, wherein to retire from time to time, to converse with Him in meekness, humility, and love. Every one is capable of such familiar conversation with God, some more, some less. (*The Practice of the Presence of God*, 7th Letter)

Although we can make a chapel of our heart and pray anywhere, it helps if we have special places that we associate with prayer. Jesus told us: 'When you pray, go into your room, close the door and pray to your Father, who is unseen. Then your Father, who sees what is done in secret, will reward you' (Matt. 6.6).

He gives this advice because he didn't want us to become hypocritical, being more concerned with how the public view our piety than concentrating on God.

As a youngster, I learnt, like many of us, to pray kneeling at my bedside before going to sleep. When I went to boarding school and had to sleep in a large dormitory, I tried to continue this practice.

My fellow boarders threw a barrage of football boots, books and anything else that was at hand at me. I felt like a martyr. But they were right. I had made a public display of praying as a witness to the faith. It was a gesture of self-righteousness.

The 'secret place' that Jesus mentions could be a corner of your home, such as a bedroom or spare room, a study or other quiet place which should provide sufficient uninterrupted privacy. You'll need to include in your prayer corner your Bible, other devotional reading and any helpful aids to meditation, such as pictures or religious articles.

It could be worthwhile to have several alternative sites. One could be out of doors: in a park, on a hillside, at the beach or beside a stream. Another location could be a favourite chapel. This need not be your local church – I've heard people say how particular churches give an aura of spirituality and prayerfulness. There is something about the history, architecture and artwork of the building that evokes a sense of the presence of God. You could choose any empty room at the office or the public library; you might even consider praying while travelling to and from work. One woman told me of how she prayed while pretending to read a newspaper or magazine on her commuter train. I usually pray while going for lengthy walks. Although I'm aware of what is going on around me, I focus on God as if he were a companion walking beside me.

Whichever places you select should help you come closer to God.

Positions

Most of us prefer to kneel or sit, a few lie prostrate, others raise their hands to heaven to pray. Some Christians dance liturgical prayers, adopt yogic positions or pray while moving through the Stations of the Cross or while saying other liturgical prayers. If you're at a church service, unless you want to stand out from the other worshippers, then the choices are normally limited to sitting, kneeling or standing – and only praying aloud if you're leading the prayers or otherwise encouraged to do so.

Does it matter what position you adopt? It's not as if you're at a crowded meeting desperately trying to attract God's attention. Yet, the posture can reflect our attitude to God.

Jesus said, 'When you stand praying . . .' (Mark 11.25), affirming that standing was the usual way of praying in his day, especially for prayers of praise and thanksgiving. Jesus also prayed lying face down before his arrest in the Garden of Gethsemane (Matt. 26.39) as a sign of his distress. Those suffering remorse for their sins sometimes did this, too, and praying while striking the breast with one's fist was a sign of repentance.

In the third century, the Desert Fathers prayed standing, facing east with cupped hands lifted to about shoulder level, symbolizing receiving the Holy Spirit, a practice many modern Christians have revived. The Celtic monks of the sixth century spent long hours standing in prayer with outstretched arms parallel to the ground in the agonizing *crossfigell* position to represent the crucified Christ. Kneeling was associated with pleading a favour from a ruler. So, early Christians kneeled when praying for people who'd led unjust and sinful lives.

In 813, the Synod of Tours demanded that all public prayers be said while kneeling, 'so that in this way we may crave God's mercy and have forgiveness of sins'. In contrast, many Protestant churches today have no facilities for kneeling since they believe that this overemphasizes our sinful nature rather than the joys of salvation. In most Orthodox churches, the few seats are for the elderly and infirm; everyone else stands or kneels. Seats, pews and kneelers are comparatively recent innovations for most Christian churches.

The idea of praying silently would seem strange to early North African Christians. They usually said their prayers aloud in a subdued voice. But some got carried away. One of their leaders, Tertullian (*c*. 155–230), had to remind his companions that megaphone prayers have no impact on God:

> Do the ears of God wait for sound? How, then, could Jonah's prayer find a way out unto heaven from the depth of the whale's belly, through the entrails of so huge a beast; from the very abysses, through so huge a mass of sea? What superior advantage will they who pray too loudly gain, except that they annoy their neighbours?
>
> (*On Prayer*, Part Third, Ethical, Chapter 17)

Tertullian emphasized that 'God is the hearer not of the voice, but of the heart'.

Many of us have learned to show respect for our Lord by bowing our heads, kneeling, genuflecting, or bowing from the waist during or before prayer. In these ways, we recognize that God is our Lord and King and that we are his dependent, humble servants. Whatever outward display you adopt, remember it's your inner attitude that counts.

No matter what your theological outlook, you will need to be realistic about the physical positions you use for personal prayer. You could make the mistake of being too comfortable. Lying in the sun on a warm day might contribute to your tan, but could prove fatal to your concentration. Snuggling up in a cosy chair before a blazing fire could be equally detrimental.

We can also go to the other extreme of deliberately making ourselves uncomfortable. In thirteenth-century Belgium, Christina the Astonishing (1150–1224) – the title is quite apt – would pray while rolling around on hot embers or while spending weeks in a freezing river. She once tied herself to a millwheel, once sat in a church font full of water and frequently prayed while balancing on a hurdle or curled up like a hedgehog on the ground. Naturally, many of the locals thought she was mad. St Patrick of Ireland (387–493) said he often prayed up to 100 prayers – probably the psalms – during the day, and again at night, in severe weather conditions:

> I used to stay out in the forests and on the mountain and I would wake up before daylight to pray in the snow, in icy coldness, in rain, and I used to feel neither ill nor any slothfulness, because, as I now see, the Spirit was burning in me at that time.
>
> (*Confessions of St Patrick*)

During the Middle Ages, some prayed while whipping themselves (flagellation) or undergoing some other kind of self-imposed ordeal to atone for their and other people's sins and show God that their prayers for forgiveness were genuine. Even today, some people subject themselves to harsh practices in the belief that this will help with their prayers. Maybe that's because we believe we need to wage war on our flesh, subduing our bodies and desires so that we can be more spiritual.

But despite Jesus' suffering and his injunction that we must take up our cross daily to follow him, we don't need to become masochists or mutilate ourselves in our efforts to reach out to God and let him touch us. Nor do we need to wage a spiritual battle with the way God created us. When Jesus said, 'God is spirit, and his worshippers must worship in spirit and in truth' (John 4.24), he was talking about our attitude to God rather than a need to beat ourselves up. We need to adopt positions that best suit our physical needs, the length of time we plan to spend in prayer, the type of prayer and, of course, where we are.

For short periods of prayer, virtually any position is possible. For longer sessions, especially for meditation and reflection, you will need to find a posture you can maintain. For most of us, this will mean sitting. Try using a padded chair with your back straight, but not rigid, feet resting on the floor and your hands held loosely in your lap. Aim to sit quite still in a relaxed manner.

If you prefer to kneel, then it might help to obtain a prayer stool or a prayer bench (prie-dieu). Make certain that what you choose is the right height for your body. You might consider using a cushion to kneel or sit upon while praying. Those who practise Zen often use a special type of cushion or *zafu*. You could vary your routine by praying while walking in a garden or park.

You could bring your hands together with the palms and inside of the outstretched fingers touching in the traditional devotional pose made famous in the *Hands of an Apostle* drawn by Albrecht Dürer (1471–1528). Or you could raise your hands heavenward. But unless you rest your arms against your body, before long you'll find that the forces of gravity can make these positions tiring for lengthy prayer.

When first taught to pray, we were encouraged to close our eyes to shut out visual distractions. The trouble with this is that the effect of keeping the eyes closed sometimes makes us more curious about what is happening around us than before. So we occasionally take a peek to see what others are doing and whether they're peeking at us. Far from helping us to concentrate on God, shutting the eyes becomes a distraction. It isn't necessary to close your eyes, but it is important that your attention be on God, not your surroundings. If shutting the eyes helps, then continue to do this. You could also try looking downward or gazing at a point in the distance. You will then be vaguely aware of what is going on around you, while your thoughts are on God.

Imagining his presence

How often have you felt God was remote from you when you prayed? You trust that he's listening, but because he isn't tangible like a normal friend you can see, hug and chat with, he doesn't seem real. As children, you might have pictured God as a wise grandfatherly figure sitting on a throne in the sky, rather like Santa Claus waiting to listen to your requests, but that doesn't work for us now.

In 1961, Yuri Gagarin (1934–68), the first person to orbit the earth in a spaceship, is supposed to have said, 'I don't see any God up here.' Transcripts of Gagarin's radio communications show he never used the phrase but, as part of a speech emphasizing the Communist Party's anti-religious views, Soviet premier Nikita Khrushchev (1894–1971) stated, 'Gagarin flew into space, but didn't see any God there.' That was not only a joke for Communists but a joke for Christians, too.

We recognize that God is everywhere and as adults we know to steer clear of the simple grandfatherly image and avoid forcing God into a human mould. We're also mindful of the second of the Ten Commandments: 'You shall not make for yourself an idol in the form of anything in heaven above or on the earth beneath or in the waters below' (Exod. 20.4). So we try to push idolatrous images of God from our thoughts. But it can be very hard to think of God in the abstract as the 'I AM WHO I AM' (Exod. 3.14) who spoke to Moses.

We really don't need to aim for theological or spiritual abstraction, and we may lose the very essence of our Christian faith by making it too sophisticated. God came among us in human form through his Son, so why not imagine that we're talking to Jesus when we pray? After all, Jesus did ask us to pray in his name, so why not imagine praying through him?

You could picture him as a counsellor, companion, colleague, or close friend – someone who's caring and prepared to listen sympathetically. Jesus taught us to pray to God as 'Our Father' as if he were a parent and he himself used the intimate 'Abba' (Mark 14.36), which is like saying 'Dad' or 'Poppa', when he prayed in the Garden of Gethsemane.

St Teresa of Avila (1515–82), who's had a major influence on our spiritual thinking over the centuries, suggested that we envisage God as either the head or a member of our family and that we vary our imagery: 'speak with him as with a father, a brother, a lord and a spouse – and, sometimes in one way and sometimes in another, he will teach you what you must do to please him' (*The Way of Perfection*, 28.3).

However you picture Jesus, don't get lost in a mass of visual detail. You could become so engrossed in the colour of his beard, his height and whether he's wearing first-century or modern clothes that your prayers become secondary. To eliminate this distraction, it's probably worth avoiding a face-to-face encounter. You could depict Jesus as the voice at the other end of the telephone, as a friend who sits just out of sight or a companion at your side. One young Christian told me that she imagines Jesus as a jogging partner. Another mentioned that whenever he has difficulty praying, he visualizes Jesus as a shadowy figure coming towards him and greeting him warmly. He then imagines them walking together along the beach or in a park.

On a holiday in Scotland, I joined a family for their Christmas meal. There were 15 people and 16 chairs. When I asked if someone was missing, they explained that the empty chair symbolized the unseen guest, who was Christ.

Since God is everywhere, he's also within us. To quote St Teresa again, 'All one need do is go into solitude and look at him within oneself, and not turn away from so good a guest but with great humility speak to him as a father' (*The Way of Perfection*, 28.2).

Although my own father died many years ago, when I think of him, I can still hear his voice and the kinds of comments he used to make. In this way, he continues to live on and direct some of my thinking. In a similar way, we can imagine Jesus' presence within us by thinking of him as an internal voice.

The New Testament refers to Jesus as the Logos or Word. John's Gospel starts, 'In the beginning was the Word, and the Word was with God, and the Word was God' (John 1.1). That's because the book of Genesis describes how God creates and controls by uttering a command. Christians relate this to the coming of Jesus in human form as the Word made flesh. Plenty of scholars have written about the concept of Logos, including Joseph Cardinal Ratzinger (1927–). Two weeks before he became Pope Benedict XVI in 2005, he gave a lecture in the convent of St Scholastica in Subiaco, Italy, in which he said:

Christianity must always remember that it is the religion of the 'Logos'. It is faith in the 'Creator Spiritus', in the Creator Spirit, from which proceeds everything that exists . . . Only creative reason, which in the crucified God is manifested as love, can really show us the way.

When you pray, perhaps you could think of God as the creative Word within you, guiding and directing you to love in a genuine, rational way.

Whether you imagine God as the Word, who's the internal voice within you, or as the human form of Jesus, avoid putting words into God's mouth. He's not an actor reciting back to you the script you've written for him, telling you the things you want to hear. To help sidestep this problem it might help to consider God as a confidant who'll listen and reflect on what you have to say, echoing your thoughts and feelings like a non-directive counsellor – but who will also challenge, encourage and support you to loving action through the power of the Holy Spirit.

Making contact

How should we begin to pray? In much the same way as we begin a conversation with anyone we love. We start by giving God our attention and tuning in to him. When Jesus taught the disciples to pray, he began: 'Our Father . . .' (Matt. 6.9–15). He focused on God, making him the subject of the prayer.

Have you ever tried to have a conversation with someone who's watching a favourite TV programme? Their mind isn't on you and, if it's important, you'll probably have to repeat the discussion at another time. Unless our attention is on God, our prayer times will become pro forma affairs: empty formalities where we go through the motions. If your prayers are to rise above the ceiling, be more than daydreaming or a monologue with yourself, then you'll need to begin by centring on God so that he can play a part in the communication.

It isn't always easy to concentrate on God. He doesn't usually stand in front of us and say, as a friend might do: 'Hi there! Haven't heard from you for a while. I'm delighted that you're looking so happy and well. Still worried about your cousin's illness, aren't you? What are your latest thoughts about changing jobs? Do tell me.' But even if

God were to do that, would we always give him our full attention? I doubt it. Even when we're with a loved one, our attention can still wander.

During his passion in the Garden of Gethsemane, Jesus pleaded with his disciples to stay awake and watch while he prayed. They started out with good intentions and then fell asleep despite Jesus waking them and reminding them of their obligations several times (Mark 14.32–41). Like the disciples, most of us find our minds meander when we begin to pray, and if we're exhausted like the disciples were, we'll nod off. A typical complaint is, 'I always start my prayers thinking about God. But I can't help thinking of my partner and the family or my shopping list, my favourite sports team and what's really bothering me. If I'm candid, I occasionally fantasize about romance and sex, so God seems to get lost in the crowd.'

Most of us plunge into prayer without taking the time to prepare ourselves. Like an athlete goes through a routine to get ready for a sports event, we, too, can benefit by going through a warm-up procedure before launching into extended periods of prayer.

The psalmist provides the key to doing this when he urges us to 'Be still, and know that I am God' (Ps. 46.10). That involves relaxing and unwinding, so that we can cast aside our daily preoccupations and centre on God. So, before launching directly into any extended periods of prayer, you might try the following warm-up exercise while sitting or lying in a comfortable position.

Begin by breathing slowly and deeply from the abdomen. Once you've established a rhythmic pattern of deep breathing, concentrate on relaxing the various parts of your body. Start with your feet, then move up to your calves, thighs, buttocks, stomach, arms, elbows and hands, then along your spine and ribs to your neck, chin, face, tongue, forehead and eyelids. Let go of all tension in your muscles until your body feels limp and heavy, as if it were detached. You may also consider yoga exercises as a warm-up procedure. If you do have trouble relaxing and your thoughts are racing on other things, you might try a warm bath before you pray – or even while you pray.

To help eliminate distractions and daily concerns that could cloud your openness to God, imagine yourself entering a tunnel that grows darker and quieter as you move further inside until at last you are alone in total darkness, alert and receptive with no intrusions, sounds or visual stimuli competing for your attention. Once you reach this stage, you are ready to give your undivided attention to God.

To fill yourself with an awareness of God's presence, picture the dark void filled with the warm light of Jesus, surrounding you and shining through your entire body so that you feel his presence around and within you. After all, Jesus did say, 'I am the light of the world' (John 8.12), but if you find this image of the light too impersonal, try imagining Jesus is somewhere there in the dark radiating a warmth and love that gradually engulfs you.

Another method of focusing on God is to concentrate on the various aspects of the Holy Trinity. Perhaps you could think of him as Creator, or else dwell on the love he has shown to us through his Son or on the continuing work of the Holy Spirit in the Church and our lives. Try not to restrict God to only one aspect of his being and way of revealing himself to us. It might be easier to consider him in terms of the historic Jesus or the present-day workings of the Holy Spirit; but to narrow God down to one short period of history is to take a lop-sided view of the Holy Trinity (see 'Imagining his presence', pp. 25–7).

Of course, we can't expect to comprehend all of the divine presence. St Paul tells us that, at best, 'we see but a poor reflection as in a mirror' (1 Cor. 13.12), but we can aim for a balanced view of God.

After practice, you'll find that you're able to centre on God without extensive preparation. Once your attention is on God and you feel that you are in his presence, ask the Holy Spirit to guide and direct you during your prayer time; then be silent and allow God to speak first.

In the same way that we might ask a friend to pray for us, Christians of some traditions will call upon a favourite saint for prayers to God on their behalf. The saint isn't a minor deity but functions as an aid to intercession.

Although Jesus told us to use his name when we make our prayer requests, so that the Father may be glorified in the Son (John 14.13), we don't have to punctuate every line with his name. It's not as though there are many gods in a heavenly open-plan office waiting to hear their individual name before they'll respond. For Christians there's only one God, and as soon as you focus on him, you have begun to pray.

Some of us still prefer to use the old-fashioned 'thees' and 'thous' when we pray, whether we pray aloud or silently in our hearts. That's because we associate this form of language with the King James Version of the Bible published in 1611 and, by implication, that must be the appropriate way to address God. Many years ago, I remember one pastor who received a reprimand from his elderly congregation for using colloquial speech and slang at public worship. They told him it was irreverent to pray to God as if he were talking with his next-door neighbour. The cleric responded by delivering the whole of his next Sunday's service, including the sermon, in Jacobean English. He'd made his point. We don't have to speak to God in one fixed form of language. Originally, the 'thou' form was used in addressing family members and close friends. To modern ears, it sounds like a relic of a bygone age and suggests a more remote formal tone. If you feel comfortable using seventeenth-century English and it helps you to be more reverent, continue to use it. It's worth remembering, though, that yesterday's aid to salvation may be today's stumbling block. So don't let these older stylized forms of speech distance you from God. The language you use should be natural, not forced.

Although we can be intimate with God, prayer is not a conversation among equals. When Jesus referred to God as 'Our Father', he highlighted that the relationship we have with him is that of child with parent. God is our Creator who provides and cares for us. That means that we, his children, need to approach him with love and respect. Jesus tells us: 'I tell you the truth, unless you change and become like little children, you will never enter the kingdom of heaven' (Matt. 18.3).

In our democratic, free-enterprise society, we've learned that success usually comes from being individualistic, self-reliant, confident and demanding. This makes it difficult for many of us to adopt a childlike attitude of humility and submission to God. We feel as if we're allowing him to bully us. Yet, in order to concentrate on God, we need to shed our pride, self-interest and demands for what we think of as our rights. The anonymous writer of the Letter to the Hebrews stresses that we all stand naked before our Lord and maker: 'Nothing in all creation is hidden from God's sight. Everything is uncovered and laid bare before the eyes of him to whom we must give account' (Heb. 4.13).

What to say

It seems odd that after Jesus had been praying in a 'certain place', the disciples asked him to teach them how to pray as John the Baptist had taught his disciples to pray (Luke 11.1). Surely, Jesus' disciples knew how to pray the psalms and other Jewish prayers on which they had been raised. What was so special about the way John had taught his followers? Did the apostles want a short cut to God that would make their prayers more effective than the customary methods?

The answer Jesus gave was a balanced approach that is God-centred, self-centred and other-centred. We repeat the Lord's Prayer so often that we almost forget what the words mean. It's worth having a look at the prayer again (see the table below).

Our Father, who art in heaven *hallowed be your name*	Greeting and praise to God who is like a parent to us. His name is blessed and holy.
Your kingdom come	Hoping for God's rule in the hearts, minds and souls of all people throughout the world.
Your will be done *On earth as it is in heaven*	Considering God's will for us, and what we will do for him to bring about his kingdom.
Give us this day our daily bread	Asking for what we most need.
And forgive us our sins, as we forgive those who sin against us	Confessing our mistakes and forgiving others who have hurt us.
And lead us not into temptation	Requesting help to avoid sin and to overcome trials to our faith.
But deliver us from evil	Appealing for help to overcome evil.
(cf. Matt. 6.9–13)	

You don't always have to merely repeat the words taught by Jesus and leave it at that. Why not use his famous prayer as a model, a guide for the content of your own prayers? Although you should begin as Jesus did by focusing on God, adoring and praising him for all the great things he can do – remember God the Father, God the

Son and God the Holy Spirit or God as Creator, Redeemer and Life Giver – there is no special reason to follow the same order. Include prayers asking that God's will be done in the world through you and others. You could ask for the Holy Spirit's guidance in all your undertakings: work, recreation, family, friends or church. You might also pray for those facing important decisions, the unconverted and those floundering with their faith. Then be ready to listen to what God wants you to do to help bring about his rule. After all, there's little point in asking that his will be done if you're not prepared to play an active part. Don't leave all of God's work to a few dedicated workers.

When Jesus mentioned our daily bread, he was referring to our everyday necessities – not luxuries. When I was a child, I prayed that God would give me a little car with an engine and lights so that I could act grown-up and be the envy of my friends. Since then, I've heard people pray for new cars, pleasure boats, and homes in upmarket neighbourhoods as well as to win sports events and lotteries. We can all rationalize why we need these things, but don't be surprised if God doesn't respond or says an emphatic 'no'. In the First Letter of John we are reminded, 'if we ask anything according to his will, he hears us' (1 John 5.14). That would rule out prayers that are little more than self-indulgent desires.

As well as praying for food and drink, employment, health, shelter, safety and companionship, include spiritual needs such as increase in faith, greater willingness to love and the ability and courage to be a better witness for Christ. We're often so busy thinking in terms of our physical necessities that we can overlook how our daily bread can include spiritual nourishment.

Jesus didn't teach us to pray for 'my daily bread' but 'our daily bread'. Our prayers should reflect a concern for the wider community, not just a few select friends. You could include prayers of intercession for the homeless, the unhappily married and those separated from a partner; unbelievers; the lonely; victims and perpetrators of crime, terror, conflict and wars; those in prison, the sick, handicapped and disabled; the hungry and those who live in poverty; and justice for the oppressed – as well as for perpetrators of injustice.

This will mean that if you are to pray effectively, you'll need to know about the real needs of people in the world, not just the sensational stories that make it to front pages or to the evening news on TV. As it's almost impossible to keep up to date with the whole spectrum of current local, national and world events, it's a good idea to concentrate on several issues and make these your special prayer concerns.

Your confessions of how you've hurt God and other people should include what you've failed to do as well as what you've done. Traditionally, we've been encouraged to think in terms of the seven deadly sins – anger, envy, avarice, pride, lust, sloth and gluttony – but don't restrict yourself to this list. There are others to do with our priorities, such as avoiding an opportunity to witness to the faith, being so busy that there was no time to pray or give someone in need your attention. Love of God and your neighbour were not your top concerns. Think about whatever has separated you from God and humbly ask for his forgiveness.

As a community, we can also offend God in the ways we treat children and the elderly, some racial and ethnic groups, social misfits, other nations and the environment. Churches can be to blame, too, especially in the way they freeze out people who don't fit into the social groupings at the local congregation or who become too troublesome. Don't forget those community sins as well.

Although confession will take up part of your prayer time, it isn't advisable to linger and wallow in self-deprecation over your mistakes. In his *Letter to Melanchthon*, Martin Luther (1483–1546), the German theologian and reformer, wrote this famous comment: 'Be a sinner and sin boldly, but believe and rejoice in Christ even more boldly, for he is victorious over sin, death, and the world.' Accept your sins are past and forgiven and that God will help to get you back on your feet when you fall in the future.

You'll also need to forgive others. This can be hard as some people have the knack of getting under our skin.

When I worked as prison psychologist in New Zealand, I counselled a man sentenced for child-molesting. He was a devout Christian and prayed for God's mercy, then wrote to the family of the girl he had sexually assaulted asking for forgiveness and offering half of his savings for her education. Although the parents were leaders in the local church, they couldn't find it in their hearts to forgive. They refused to have anything more to do with this first-time offender and demanded retribution from the state. His sentence, they complained, was too light. They wanted him castrated. When I told this story on a New Zealand radio network as an example of someone who was trying to make amends for what he had done wrong, the switchboard was quickly jammed with callers demanding a law change to enable castration for paedophiles and that we lock them up and throw away the key.

To dramatize the importance of forgiving others, Jesus told a similar story of an unforgiving debtor and instructed us to forgive 77 times and to turn the other cheek (Matt. 18.21–35). He also forgave those who crucified him (Luke 23.34).

Most of us are aware of our weaknesses and of what tempts us away from God. When you examine your sins, take note of how you strayed and ask for God's help in avoiding these situations. If gluttony is a problem, tell God about your addiction to food, drink or both, and ask for strength and guidance in overcoming this temptation. Be open to God's direction, especially through the wisdom of others. The first move might be to get medical advice or join a support group.

It's worth bearing in mind what St Paul tells us: that God sometimes puts temptation in our way to test our faith. But he assures us that, through God's grace, we will be strengthened and able to meet the challenge.

> No temptation has seized you except what is common to man. And God is faithful; he will not let you be tempted beyond what you can bear. But when you are tempted, he will also provide a way out so that you can stand up under it. (1 Cor. 10.13)

People have different ideas about the existence of an evil one or a devil. But whatever your stand on this issue, we can agree that there's evil in the world. There are tragic accidents, illness and disease, pollution and terrible natural disasters, as well as the horrific inhumanity we inflict on one another. Christians have even been guilty of appalling cruelty and violence in the name of Christ.

We can find it difficult to cope with these evils. So, instead, we try to deny evil and what we can do to help overcome it by complaining of how the media keeps feeding us negative images, or else we shut our eyes in the hope they will go away. It's as if we want to escape to an imaginary Garden of Eden and pretend that the Fall never happened. But Jesus didn't ignore those suffering the consequences of evil. Nor did he escape from his passion in the Garden of Gethsemane, and neither should we shut ourselves off from understanding evil. Those involved need our prayers.

As our own attitudes can contribute to evil, you will need to take a good look at yourself. Do you get a vicarious thrill out of watching violent television programmes? What are your thoughts on armed intervention? Surveys in the USA in 2003 found that despite most church organizations and leaders being against going to war with Iraq, Christians in the pews were slightly more in favour of the war than the general population (nearly two-thirds of the population). This was played on by the administration and there are now tens of thousands of casualties from that war – and its effects are ongoing.

Do you drive recklessly, endangering the lives of other people? You might think that's not even worth mentioning compared to the atrocities committed by Hitler, Stalin, Pol Pot or the terror tactics of Osama bin Laden. Nevertheless, hundreds of thousands of people die and are maimed in vehicle accidents caused by careless driving.

That means you need to be open to the possibility of being an instrument of evil. On a world scale, your contribution might look minute but cumulatively it all adds up.

Whatever you pray for, you will need to be specific. If we pray for everything in general, we pray for nothing in particular. On the other hand, if we are too detailed, we can border on the ridiculous, asking God to decide on trivial matters – like finding you a parking space near the local shopping centre – which can have little to do with his kingdom.

Another popular prayer model has the acronym ACTS. This stands for adoration, confession, thanksgiving and supplication (prayers of request). All four elements of ACTS, with the possible exception of thanksgiving, are included in the discussion on the Lord's Prayer (of course, praise and adoration can imply thanksgiving). It's a good idea to give special thanks to God. When Jesus healed the ten lepers, only one returned to thank him (Luke 17.12–19). The rest forgot. Many Jewish prayers, including those of Jesus' time, are of praise and thanksgiving. So, avoid taking God for granted.

If you can't think of anything to say to God, don't let this worry you or give up. 'In the same way, the Spirit helps us in our weakness. We do not know what we ought to pray for,' St Paul assures us, 'but the Spirit himself intercedes for us with groans that words cannot express. And he who searches our hearts knows the mind of the Spirit, because the Spirit intercedes for the saints in accordance with God's will' (Rom. 8.26–27). Just being with God could be your prayer.

Which method?

There are many prayer methods. It's a question of finding the most appropriate style for you. Some methods take fleeting moments, some last for an entire weekend or many days. Other methods require meditating on the Gospel or wordless contemplation. Prayer may include letter-writing, singing, glossolalia (speaking in tongues), the rosary, group meditation, mantras and even watching television. Much of the rest of this book is devoted to explaining these methods.

Maybe you use some of these techniques already and feel hesitant about trying something different, especially if it's from outside your prayer tradition. Some of us become uneasy at the mention of the rosary, praying in tongues, the constant repetition of a mantra like the Jesus Prayer, or mysticism. Often that's because we don't understand what's involved or we associate the prayer style with a branch of the Church with which we have differences. But don't be so defensive that you dismiss other methods out of hand. You could be blocking off worthwhile avenues to God.

One man told me that all he had to do to pray was sit down and start talking to God. He was implying that was all there was to it. 'That's great,' I replied. 'Do you communicate with your partner by talk alone? Don't you sometimes write emails, text or telephone her, go for walks or dance together, touch her lovingly or just be silent enjoying each other's company?' He realized what I was getting at. There's more than one way of approaching God and we need to be flexible.

This doesn't mean that we should swing to the other extreme and rush into all the methods at once. They're only a means to an end, a way of reaching out to make contact. Some people, including the saints who specialized in prayer, talk as if some methods are for learners and other methods, especially contemplative and mystical styles, are more advanced. That's a mistake. It's a snobbish attempt to put the prayers of the contemplative on a pedestal. They're just different methods. Contact should be your priority. You're not trying to rack up points on a heavenly scoreboard by impressing God with your spiritual expertise.

Another hazard is discussing and theorizing about prayer but never getting around to actually praying. Jesus didn't ask us to be armchair commentators. He wants us to pray. That means learning about prayer firsthand.

Treat this book as you would a cookbook of recipes. After flicking through the pages, you could select one or two methods that either build on what you are already doing or are new to you and work with them for a while before moving on to another technique. You might tailor these methods to your individual circumstances. Be patient but don't stick with a method if it's hindering communication with God. Whatever method you adopt, I hope it helps enrich your prayer life.

3

PRAYER
IN YOUR OWN WORDS

Cries from the heart

When the psalmist wrote: 'The LORD is near to all who call on him, to all who call on him in truth' (Ps. 145.18), he was affirming that God is willing to listen to anyone who calls out to him in sincerity. That means you don't have to have a prepared speech. Nor do your prayers have to be in sentences or be comprehensible to others.

We strive so often to imitate the prayers of the experts that we can turn our own prayer into an intellectual exercise that lacks depth of feeling and passion. We pray from our heads rather than from our hearts. But God doesn't want us to have a polite conversation with him that has no heart or passion. He expects honest, no-holds-barred, warts-and-all prayers that express what you really think and feel: 'pour out your heart like water in the presence of the Lord' (Lam. 2.19).

Sometimes we feel so emotionally moved that all we can do is utter a simple exclamation like 'Fantastic!' or 'How dreadful!' These utterances convey a depth of feeling and meaning, so why not treat them as prayers to God?

After hearing of her daughter's serious injuries in a car accident, all one woman could say as she rushed to be by her daughter's side was, 'Oh God! My God! Please, please, be with her!' She repeated the words, aloud and to herself, over and over. Everything she felt was in that prayer – her love for her daughter, her anxiety and concern, as well as her simple request to God.

Of course, you don't have to wait for a crisis. You can use a cry just as effectively on other occasions: when you feel happy, in love, upon the birth of a child or when you are overwhelmed by the magnificence of nature. Before visiting the Grand Canyon, I cynically thought its grandeur had been over-hyped. I was wrong. It was the middle of winter and the snow added to the awesome splendour of this natural wonder. All I could say was, 'What a creation! Thanks, God!' Others might say 'Hallelujah!', 'Praise the Lord!' or 'Good God!' These joyous cries all suggest the same thing – praising and thanking God for his magnificent creation.

If you're anxious, frightened, angry, annoyed about a mistake, lonely or suffering from the pangs of guilt, think of these negative feelings as prayers. A plain 'I've sinned', 'Lord, I've messed up' or

'Oh God!' can convey the depth of your feelings to God. They're your prayers, pure and simple.

Don't be put off using these spontaneous cries to God because so many people use the names of God and Jesus when they curse and swear. When you say 'Jesus Christ' or 'Oh God', it doesn't mean that you're automatically uttering a profanity. God forbid! It depends on your intentions. If you're worried that those who overhear you might misunderstand you, then a silent cry is just as effective.

Many dedicated Christians, including mystics who've devoted their lives to prayer, use this simple prayer method. In a few utterances, they focus all their feelings, emotions and intellect on God. One of the early Desert Fathers and Scythian monks from what is now Romania, St John Cassian (*c.* 360–433), encouraged fellow monks to frequently pray the cry of the psalmist, 'Hasten, O God, to save me; O LORD, come quickly to help me' (Ps. 70.1). The twentieth-century Italian mystic, Padre Pio (1887–1968), constantly repeated the words *Gesú, Maria* – Jesus, Mary – as he lay on his deathbed. Others might exclaim: 'God be praised', 'Amen' or '*Maranatha*' – 'Come, Lord Jesus.' These words are not trite expressions, but are packed with meaning and associations. A short, spontaneous utterance can be the most effective of prayers. For if one cry from the heart can say it all, why be long-winded?

One-liners

When working as a journalist, I often asked people I was interviewing, 'Imagine you're in an elevator with me for three floors and that's all the time you've got to get your main points across. What would you tell me?' That would help concentrate their thinking to what mattered so that they were able to give a worthwhile sound bite. It's a good approach to prayer, too.

If you've a few moments to spare – while stopped at traffic lights, waiting for a bus, rocking a child to sleep, at a boring meeting or standing in an elevator – why not compose a simple prayer? It need only be a one-line sentence – or even a question to God. It's like sending a text message. You have one or two points and you make them briefly. Unlike a cry from the heart, which is more of a spontaneous emotional outpouring, one-liners reflect your thoughts. They're more of a planned head response than a gut reaction.

At a wedding reception, I said the following grace, 'Thank you, Lord, for this happy occasion and for the food we're about to eat. Amen.' Everyone burst out laughing and made comments like, 'You must be very hungry to give us such a short prayer.' They expected that, as a clergyperson, I should have produced something more erudite and profound. What they didn't seem to realize was that what matters is not the number of words we offer to God but the sincerity of those words.

When his barber and friend of many years, Peter Beskendorf, asked the German theologian and reformer, Martin Luther, for guidelines on how to pray, Luther wrote his popular: *How One Should Pray, for Master Peter the Barber* or, as it is usually titled, *A Simple Way to Pray*. Luther maintains that with lengthy prayers we're apt to babble while our minds wander: 'A person who forgets what he has said has not prayed well. In a good prayer, one fully remembers every word and thought from the beginning to the end of the prayer.' Instead, on the principle that quality is better than quantity, he advises that short frequent prayers are best: 'A good prayer should not be lengthy or drawn out, but frequent and ardent.'

You can turn practically anything into a short prayer. It can be the boss at work, a crying baby, a nostalgic memory, a news story, a pound coin, the police officer who just passed you in a patrol car, the homeless person or a trip to a supermarket.

Once in a supermarket I had my eye on a packet of fancy biscuits. I really didn't need them but they did look enticing as advertisements of how 'I deserved a little luxury now and then' played subliminally in my brain. I thought of an appropriate prayer and before I had finished uttering, 'Thank you, God, for our daily bread' (because it was hard on the spur of the moment to formulate a prayer that wasn't a rationalization in favour of those biscuits), I had my answer. My daily bread was already in the shopping basket. So I thought of others who were not so fortunate and put the money aside for hunger relief. This story raises another point about one-liners. In thinking about what to say, you're listening to God as well. In his advice to his barber, Luther advocated listening to God in the thoughts we have while we pray: 'One word of his [the Holy Spirit's] sermon is far better than a thousand of our prayers. Many times I have learned more from one prayer than I might have learned from much reading and speculation.'

You never know what God might want to say.

Your prayer-sentences don't always have to be statements. We often ask questions throughout the day, so why not ask questions of God? While surfing the Internet, perhaps you could ask, 'What sites would be best for me to visit, Lord?' Once you've raised this question, it's surprising how your criteria for Internet sites changes. You can hardly be serious about your question if you choose a steady diet of pornography and violent games.

If you're worried about your kids' behaviour, why not form a sentence like, 'Show me, heavenly Father, how to set them a loving example'? If you see an ambulance speeding by, instead of being annoyed at having to pull over, why not say a prayer for the victim or give brief thanks for the paramedics?

When you're going through a dry spell during your scheduled prayer time, one-liners are an ideal way of keeping your prayer life alive. You can offer any of your thoughts as an instant prayer, even your antisocial fantasies. If you think your boss is unfair, quick to blame you or your colleagues for anything that goes wrong and eager to take the credit for anything that's good, why not offer a short prayer like this: 'I can't stand my boss, help me to deal with this person'? One man who did this had a mental image of Jesus dying on the cross for all people, including his persecutors. He realized that Jesus' loving sacrifice extended to his boss as well as himself. And that gave him the courage to confront his boss with her management style and make positive suggestions.

By using short prayers – sometimes called arrow prayers, ejaculatory prayers or aspirations – you can keep in touch with God throughout the day. This makes it possible; even if you're very busy, to begin to fulfil Jesus and St Paul's advice to pray constantly.

Saying more

Have you ever noticed how teenagers who send dozens of text messages to one another also spend plenty of time chatting over the phone and meeting with one another as well? Much the same can happen with our prayer life. The more we make contact with God, the more we'll want to make contact.

That means there'll be plenty of times when you'll need to pray more than a sentence or two – especially if there's heaps on your mind. You might want to say a lot about your relationship with your partner – or your lack of one – the crime rate, injustices you know of, unemployment, your concerns about health issues, the local church, or to give thanks to God for his many blessings. Moreover, few of us are so saintly that we could reduce our confessions to a plaintive cry or a one-liner.

Having much to say is one thing, but being able to say it is quite another. Many of us dry up when we approach God in prayer. After the first couple of sentences, we seem to run out of gas or go off on a tangent and never get round to saying what's on the tip of our tongues. Or else we flinch at the thought of telling God the truth. This is a familiar problem. Roman playwright and Stoic philosopher Lucius Annaeus Seneca (*c.* 4 BC–AD 65) wrote about it in a letter towards the end of his life: 'We often want one thing and pray for another, not telling the truth even to the gods.'

It's similar to what used to happen when I first placed international calls home to New Zealand while a student in England. After the initial excited greeting, neither party knew quite what to say next. Before the call, my mind was crammed with things to say but once I made contact they seemed to evaporate. Instead, my parents and I talked about the weather like familiar strangers. In those days international telephone calls were very expensive, so it didn't take long to realize that, in future, I would need to have a few notes at hand if I wanted to avoid unnecessary meteorological discussions.

The same procedure can be used to avoid being at a loss for words while communicating with God. Unless you have a good memory, why not jot down prayer points in a notepad, on your computer or palmtop? This will help jog your memory and prepare you for what you want to discuss with God. Once you have a list, you can develop your thoughts into lengthier prayer conversations.

Check your notes and recall details. Don't be vague. Martin Luther reminds his readers in his *A Simple Way to Pray* of the proverb: *Pluribus intentus, minor est ad singula sensus* – 'He who thinks of many things, thinks of nothing and does nothing right.' So avoid rambling promiscuous prayer. Be specific. If you made a note to give thanks for your job, then you could associate this with your income, talents, health and the companionship of each of your colleagues – mentioning particulars. You might also think in terms of how your work is contributing to the welfare of the community, and give thanks to God. You could then think of the work of others. Perhaps you could pray for workers in your neighbourhood, unions and management associations, including particular people and their attitudes, honesty at work, industrial safety, the unemployed, the under-employed and those who are unhappy in their work. In this way, you extend your prayers to others, even if you started with yourself.

Once associations spring to mind around a particular point, you'll soon find that you'll have plenty to chat about to God. So don't feel you have to continue with your list if you find that you're being inspired by the Holy Spirit over one point. God often speaks through your thoughts and you don't want to cut him off because you're in a hurry to get through all your prayer points in one session.

Once you've outlined the situation to God, you can then ask for his guidance. Be ready for the Holy Spirit to lead you. This might take the form of suggesting a new safety procedure, befriending that unhappy co-worker or raising policy issues over minorities and business ethics.

You can treat most topics in a similar way. If you have noted a tendency to stuff yourself with junk food, begin your prayer by mentioning when and what you overeat, the likely consequences to your health, how this could affect your responsibilities and why you think you give in to this temptation. Then ask for God's help and guidance about weight control programmes, medical help, counselling and other steps you might take. When you broaden your associations, you could pray about obesity, malnutrition, the two-thirds of the world that suffer from hunger, those who work to solve these problems and the availability of good food for you. This will put your temptation into a wider perspective so that you can be more open to the direction of the Holy Spirit. But don't dwell on your temptations. Revisiting them many times gives them power over you by making them seem insurmountable. Trust in God to help you find an answer.

You don't need to pray about serious things only. We often joke, make humorous comments and exaggerate issues for a laugh with those we love. It's a way of coping with problems and bonding with others. So, as long as you're respectful, why not do the same with your prayers. 'Lord, I forgive those who've done wrong to me – as long as they're nice to me from now on', brings a smile, because it's honest. It's also a way of saying to God that you fall short and need his help in extending forgiveness to those who're hard to forgive.

It's worth keeping your notes. They can serve as a prayer outline for other occasions. Check that your prayers are balanced; remember to include adoration, confession, thanksgiving and supplication (see 'What to say', p. 35). Other material can also act as a stimulus to prayer: the Bible, the Apostles' Creed or Nicene Creed, the Lord's Prayer, religious icons and art, the rosary, music, nature. You'll find discussion and advice on how to use these prompts throughout this book. You could also think of exchanging your outlines with other Christians so that you can learn much from one another.

Media prayer

Turn your television viewing into a time of prayer. A shocking news story, a dramatic presentation – even the commercials – can be included in your prayers. That'll transform you from a passive viewer to an active prayerful participant. The influential Swiss Protestant theologian, Karl Barth (1886–1968), maintained: 'God is to be found in two main ways: in his Word, and in other words. The Christian in daily life should go forth, the Bible in one hand and the daily newspaper in the other.' That also applies to our prayers. We can use the Bible for inspiration but we're limiting the relevance and power of our prayer if we cut ourselves off from our surroundings and the kind of action needed to bring about a positive change.

The procedure's simple. First, watch a programme and absorb what's going on. Effective prayer requires that you're well informed. Then pray for all involved. Next, think of similar situations and include them in your prayers. Finally, give thanks or ask God for guidance.

Suppose an act of terrorism features on the news. As the victims, the response of the authorities, the suspects and their motives are revealed, mention them in a short prayer. Don't let the plight of the victims close your mind to the problems of the attackers. Many acts of terrorism are a desperate effort to draw attention to what the perpetrators believe is an act of injustice, especially domination by an occupying power. Though their methods have tragic consequences for innocent victims and their families, God cares about everyone. Pray for a just and peaceful settlement and ask God how he can use you to help bring that about. Don't be surprised if God expects you to do some extraordinary things that seem beyond your capabilities. It was in praying a prayer like that, that I became a journalist – despite having dyslexia – reporting and making documentaries on international conflicts in an effort to inform people.

A nature documentary can receive the same prayer treatment. Here, you might pray for the forms of life portrayed and the specialists concerned with research for their preservation. You could then praise God for the wonder of his creation and ask for direction in treating his creation wisely. Maybe you'll think again about buying a big gas-guzzling four-wheel-drive vehicle and opt for a hybrid fuel vehicle, replace incandescent light bulbs with low-energy ones or buy carbon credits to offset necessary air travel; or even question whether buying carbon credits is the modern-day equivalent of the medieval practice of buying sin indulgences from the Church.

Insofar as television dramas and advertising mirror contemporary life and values, we can also turn to them as a source of prayer. If the routine fare of dramatized violence, sex, exploitation and materialism disgusts you, pray about this and switch channels. An aspirin advertisement might stimulate prayers for human suffering and relief, but you could also use the timeout for the sponsor's message as a mini-meditation or prayer period.

You can use the same techniques while listening to the radio, reading a newspaper or when downloading news from the Internet or your cell phone. Many Christians have told me that they make their intercessions while following the news on their car radio. The big advantage of the print medium and news and commentaries on the Internet is that you can refer again to the material and share it with others.

Perhaps you might put clippings and downloaded articles in a physical or e-scrapbook especially for prayer.

The scrapbook

Most of us collect photos, clippings, cards, poems and anything else that makes a strong impression on us. You could just as easily create an album to prompt you to pray. This would be your own distinctive prayer book. Start with an empty book – or blank document on your computer – and add whatever will lead you to think of God.

Don't think that you have to stick to postcard reproductions of Leonardo da Vinci's *The Last Supper* or El Greco's rendition of Jesus at the crucifixion site in a scarlet robe in his *The Disrobing of Christ*. My personal collection is an eclectic one – photographs of the family, godchildren, friends, my home, people I've met and places I've visited throughout the world. It also contains postcards of Christian art and architecture; baptism, confirmation and ordination certificates; Christmas and birthday cards; letters; prayers and quotations; religious jokes and cartoons; an olive leaf from the Garden of Gethsemane and a palm cross made for me by a small boy on an oasis in the Sahara Desert.

But my prompts to prayer aren't limited to a scrapbook. There are copies of Greek and Russian icons on my walls, along with a scene of the Last Supper painted with ordinary enamel house paint by an artist who'd lost his home and family and had sought sanctuary in a church refugee centre in El Salvador during the 1980–92 civil war. Every time I look at that, I give thanks for the Eucharist and meditate on how Christ's body is broken for all of us, including the marginalized and those who persecute and do harm.

I also have a priest's chasuble painstakingly made for me on a backstrap loom by a Mam Indian woman in the highlands of Guatemala. The military junta had set fire to her village and most of its inhabitants were tortured or killed in the genocide committed against the Indians, which finally ended in 1996. She had taken in her young niece, the sole survivor of her brother's family. Despite the extra mouth to feed and her extreme poverty, this woman made my chasuble as a prayer and gift to God. Weaving experts tell me it's among the finest weaving they've seen. I paid her much more than the price she asked for the four months of hard work and she received my money a week after she learned she had cancer of the womb. The extra I paid enabled her to have a life-saving operation that she could otherwise never afford. She praised God for answering her prayers and for blessing her. Every time I put that chasuble on to celebrate the Eucharist, I become part of that prayer. I automatically feel humbled by her faith, fired by the Holy Spirit to work for justice and peace, and thankful to God.

Other Christians have used their fridge doors as a bulletin board for prayers, which helps make prayer a family affair. They've included pictures of their pets, a patron saint, photos of people they're praying for, copies of prayer requests from individuals or groups and their own religious artwork. One person I know carries around a horseshoe nail in his pocket as a constant reminder of Jesus' crucifixion and his need to praise and thank God for this selfless act of love.

You can use your scrapbook and other triggers for prayer in much the same way as prayer notes or media stories. Let your mementos act as a stimulus to prayer. Pick a subject and make specific associations. Your own baptismal certificate could promote meditation and prayer about being born anew in Jesus Christ and then extended to those you're a godparent to or those you know who've recently been baptized. A photograph of old friends could elicit prayers for their present well-being. On the other hand, a palm cross, an icon or a religious artwork could be the basis for a sustained in-depth meditation.

Letters to God

Have you ever had the experience of thinking that you knew a friend until you received his or her first letter? A letter can open a new window into their personality. Someone you thought was relatively humourless can turn out pages of witty prose, while a friend who's reticent about offering an opinion in a group can be quite forthright on paper or in an email. Letters enable people to express themselves differently and to raise subjects, thoughts and feelings they might find difficult to mention face to face. That's why Internet chat rooms are so popular. Internet users can remain anonymous by using a pen name so they can say what they feel without any comebacks. It may also explain why many people send their prayers to Web addresses where groups of devout Christians will pray for them.

Unlike a casual conversation, a letter shows that you've made a special effort for the recipient. It's a permanent record that can be reread and shared with others. Many parish prayer groups, or prayer-trees, use email to forward prayers to one another. It's a highly efficient and cost-effective way of making prayer requests known.

While studying at Oxford, my future first wife (who has since died) and I conducted a three-year courtship by regular mail as there was no email in those days. Although separated by 19,000 kilometres, we were able to remain close in spirit. For many years after our marriage, we enjoyed corresponding when we were apart. It gave time to think about what we really wanted to say, knowing that the other partner was going to reread and savour the words.

Yet, when it comes to writing to God, most of us still think twice before tapping out a message on the keyboard or putting pen to paper. Many of us suffer writer's block or feel that our writing isn't up to God's standard – as if he's a grammar teacher who's going to give an A+ down to an F grade on our efforts or not bother to read our letters.

People who've written letters to God confirm that this adds a new dimension to their prayer life. Instead of blurting out whatever comes to mind, they can develop more fully their innermost thoughts and feelings. The procedure is the same as writing to anyone you dearly love. After opening with your greetings, spell out what is really on your mind. Don't feel you have to rival St Paul and write a massive epistle. There are postcards and text-message letters, too. I remember one man who was very inarticulate to whom I suggested writing God a postcard. He conscientiously laboured over each phrase, but the result was worth the effort. He succeeded in expressing exactly what he felt.

Dear God

I'm glad you love me. I love you, too. I don't always know how to say things but I feel them anyhow. Thank you for what you've done for me.

Your true friend

Ron

Another man poured out his anger in this letter:

God

If you love people as much as you say you do, why did you let those ten people die in that terrible fire yesterday? Bystanders heard their screams and were powerless to save them. God! What an awful way to go. How could you allow it to happen? I would do everything possible to help my children in a fire. If we're all your children, why didn't you do something?

After several more pages describing other tragedies, he told God he couldn't see any point in continuing the relationship. He'd produced the proverbial Dear John letter and, like many such letters, he rewrote it. In the first draft, he vented his anger. Once he'd calmed down, he started to reflect on Christ's sacrifice and love. He hadn't had his question answered of why God didn't do anything to save the victims but he felt he could trust again in God's love.

It might seem presumptuous to imagine how God would answer. Yet, we can sometimes learn about his will for us if we attempt a reply. After you've written your letter to God, pray for the Holy Spirit's guidance in answering it. Don't feel you have to respond right away. It usually pays to wait several days.

You mustn't automatically assume the answer you write is the Holy Spirit working in you and therefore God's will. But it can provide valuable insights. Be prepared for surprises. As she began a reply to her letter, one woman was startled to see God greeting her by name and thanking her for writing. She knew in theory that God loves and cares for each of us, but it hadn't hit home until she saw it written out. Some, who could not truly accept God's forgiveness until they had set it down on paper with their own name mentioned, report a similar experience.

Keep a file of your correspondence for future reference. It's a record of your relationship with God and how you understand him to be active in your life (see 'Keeping in touch', pp. 178–80).

Poetry and song

Once I heard a radio talk show where the topic was 'your poetry'. Within minutes, the switchboard was jammed with callers eager to share their heart-wrenching verse on family, pets, love, loss and all their innermost feelings. The art of writing poetry is obviously alive and well and isn't the exclusive domain of pretentious Bohemian intellectuals.

During a university vacation, I worked in the Post Office alongside one of New Zealand's best-known poets, James K. Baxter (1926–72). It was interesting to see him in action. I naively thought that, unlike the rest of us, good poets could look at something or have a strong impression of something and the words would then flow naturally – as some modern rap poets do. Nothing could be further from the truth. He did have moments of inspiration where the words flowed quickly but, mostly, he struggled to find the right metaphor. He would ask questions like, 'What does this particular leaf mean to you?' or 'How do you picture God when you pray?' He was constantly searching for images and allegories everyone could understand.

You could be a budding poet yourself, so why not consider turning your talents to poems or hymns to God? It's a good way of concentrating your thoughts to focus on what you really feel about him as you search for the metaphors to express what you want to say. All the devices of the poet are at your disposal: imagery, simile, allusion, alliteration, assonance, irony, humour and puns. You might consider using the established formats of a sonnet, elegy – or even a limerick or the short Japanese poem style of haiku. Your poems don't have to rhyme; they could be free verse. Here's a poem I recently wrote.

> God, it's hard to communicate.
> You're like a date leaving me waiting
> in suspense
> at the door pacing up and down
> full of love and hope
> without pretence
> wondering what to anticipate.
>
> Time passes, you don't appear.
> I'll knock again
> call out,
> in case you haven't heard.
> I'm here patient, expectant
> without doubt.
> Surely, you can lend me an ear.
>
> What are you doing
> that takes so long?
> I stand here
> pensive and anxious.
> You promised. Did I do wrong?
> Are you near,
> deaf or tardy?
> Playing hard to get?
> Your silence leaves me fuming.

My passion's wilted.
You stood me up.
Our date is off.
A lonely soliloquy at your door;
nothing more.
You said nought, not a cough.
I haven't a chance
not a prayer.
I guess I'm jilted.

I'll try another day.
Perhaps I'm not forsaken.
Lovers who persevere, they say,
can win a distant heart
when prospects look bleak
and their day turns to dark night
if they don't fall apart
have faith
and don't stray.

Knock, knock, it's me again.
Don't keep me in suspense.
This time
answer with a smile,
apologize for last time
but you're not obliged.
I'll stay awhile
trying yet again
until we reach an 'Amen'.

Most children and teenagers go through a phase of expressing themselves in verse. Whenever I have asked a church youth group to contribute prayers to a parish magazine, they inevitably write poetry. These days, the rap-style Christian hip-hop or Christ-hop is popular. Here's an example of one I wrote for a friend.

Preacher said it right
In a sound bite
I'm one crude dude
who treats you rude
Gotta say thanks
Praise ya to the sky
Cause you're the BIG GUY.

You could try turning your prayer-poems into songs or hymns. You don't have to be a composer. You could team up with someone who is or write your own lyrics to an existing tune. If you plan to perform the music in public, check the copyright. Old favourites like 'The Old Hundredth', 'Jesu, Joy of Man's Desiring', or 'Faith of Our Fathers' and traditional folk tunes are often set to alternative texts and have the advantage of being in the public domain.

You could consider adding to the musical repertoire of your local church by contributing original verses for special occasions. Even if appropriate hymns are available, a setting of your own words at a wedding, baptism, anniversary or funeral could make the ceremony more personal and a chance to share your prayers with others.

When others say it better

Other people's prayers can express what we want to say to God. Their language and emphasis will be different from ours and this can inspire our own prayers.

Many years ago when I first read Michel Quoist's *Prayers of Life*, I was struck by a prayer entitled 'The Bald Head'. All the prayers I'd heard up to that stage had been far more stylized and traditional in their approach. It would never have occurred to me to make a hairless head the subject of a prayer. But Abbé Quoist (1921–97), sitting behind a bald man at a boring lecture, associated this with a quote of Jesus: 'Not a hair of your head will perish' (Luke 21.18) and created a prayer on God's unique love.

Malcolm Boyd (1923–), a social activist who became known as 'the espresso priest' for his religious poetry readings at a San Francisco nightclub, has also shown us how we can draw on everyday experience. His social commentary prayers in *Are You Running with Me, Jesus?* – and similar books – include topics and an approach you're not likely to hear at a local church prayer meeting. Nevertheless, they do reflect what's on many people's minds, especially young people: reflections on films, sexual freedom, a gay bar, an empty house, loneliness and racial attitudes. These reflections gave me a new perspective of what we can include in prayer: anything and everything that's on our minds.

Some people have the gift of expressing thoughts and feelings to God much better than we can. Most of us never tire of rereading or singing well-known prayers such as the Peace Prayer, wrongly attributed to St Francis of Assisi (see 'The close-up', p. 89), or this 1548 Prayer of Generosity by St Ignatius of Loyola:

Teach us, good Lord, to serve thee as thou deservest:
To give and not to count the cost;
To fight and not to heed the wounds;
To toil and not to seek for rest;
To labour and not to ask for any reward
Save that of knowing that we do thy will.

Or take this popular example from the 1558 *Old Sarum Primer*:

God be in my head,
And in my understanding;
God be in my eyes,
And in my looking;
God be in my mouth,
And in my speaking;
God be in my heart,
And in my thinking;
God be at my end,
And at my departing.

You might consider making personal additions or adapting existing prayers. In the above example, you could insert:

God be in my ears,
And in my listening;
God be in my hands,
And in my working.

Most of us have our personal favourites. I particularly like the sonnet 'Batter my heart, three person'd God' by John Donne (1572–1631), the psalms – including those psalms which ask God to strike the enemy, as they express how we can sometimes feel – and many of the prayers of Augustinian monk Thomas à Kempis (1380–1471) in *The Imitation of Christ*. You will have your own preferences, but don't limit yourself to these. If you expose yourself to a wide range of writers, their prayers will help balance the content of your own.

There are plenty of published collections, including liturgical prayer books and missals. Some of the hymns and songs we sing make good prayers, while the Bible, especially the Psalter and John's Gospel, is another rich source. And, of course, there're hundreds of thousands of Internet sites featuring daily prayers and Bible readings. Most mainstream church organizations have their own daily prayer services on the Internet. Otherwise, just put the words 'daily prayer' into a search engine and pick the style of prayers that you're looking for. Be warned, though, that when I did this, I got over three and a half million sites. So, it would be best to make your search more specific, like 'Daily Anglican prayers and lectionary', 'Daily Roman Catholic office', 'Prayers at a time of loss', 'Traditional prayers of praise and thanksgiving', or 'Prayers for my family' (see 'Further reading' for some key Internet resources). If you feel in a jovial mood, you might even want to look up some humorous prayers. Many people stick with one favourite website as they feel part of that site's invisible praying 'congregation' in cyberspace.

Other people's prayers can help in times of spiritual dryness. They can give you a wealth of material to fall back on when you are stuck for words. For this reason, Christians of some traditions lay great emphasis on memorized prayers. When you use someone else's prayer, take it slowly. Don't rush. We've all heard those charge-of-the-light-brigade recitations when no one has time to pause or reflect. Like the original Charge of the Light Brigade at the Battle of Balaclava during the Crimean War, they have little impact. Think about the meaning of the words. Let them become your words.

57

4

DECISION-MAKING
AND HEALING

Making decisions

Your choice of career, which college to attend, whether to get married, where to live or how to make a tough ethical choice – these are major decisions, and hard to make.

Sometimes a simple question to God can uncover the right decision (see 'One-liners', pp. 42–4). But if the problem seems complex and you can see no simple answer, the following procedure may be helpful in allowing God to work through your intellect, heart and conscience as well as your attitudes and actions.

First, tell God what you are trying to decide and ask for his guidance in making this choice so that the choice is according to his will.

Now, create a 'Decision-making table' as shown on pp. 62–3. You can do this on a computer table or spreadsheet or on paper.

Begin by jotting down all the relevant points you can think of in the 'Information' column. That will include what you now think of as positive, negative or neutral information. Some people prefer to produce 'for' and 'against' tables listing the pros and cons and then compare the two. That assumes, though, that you already know what information is positive, what's negative, and how to compare them.

For some issues you may need to do further research to get more information. Ask friends and the relevant experts, read articles, books and search the Internet. Find out as much as you can about each of the alternatives you're considering. For example, if you're trying to make up your mind whether to go into journalism or the computer field, check on what's involved in each type of work – hours, salary, contact with people and scope for challenge and growth. Then look at whether you have the talents or could acquire the necessary skills and qualifications and have the ability and resources to do so, whether your personality is suited for the work, what the opportunities are, how long it takes to train and how much competition there is in the job market.

If it's the ethical question of your 17-year-old daughter wanting to bring her boyfriend home to sleep in her room, you may like to hear what she has to say, including comments like, 'You're treating me like a little kid. Would you rather we did it in the back seat of the car? We have a different attitude to sex than you do.' You might also enter your desire for her to respect your values in your home, and so on.

Decision-making table

Sample: whether to marry your boyfriend or girlfriend

Information	Rank whether it fits your goals and values	Challenges and risks High, medium, low	Actions	What your heart and conscience say
Physical attraction	3	May not last beyond honeymoon period	Recognize that, while important, our relationship needs grounding in common interests, religious faith, compatible personality, friendship	Feel good when we're close. But this could be because of familiarity and it could be the same with another in the future
Great friends	1	Low risk of change	Continue to enjoy and support this	Although there's a great friendship, we do have differences over important religious, political and ethical issues
Common interests	2	Mainly sport and work. High risk of that changing in next ten years, putting strain on relationship	Check to see what other interests we have in common. Maybe suggest something new	Feel that in ten years, we won't have much in common, unless we still have mutual interests
Approval of family	4	High chance that's because family and friends like my partner, not because it's best for both of us	Do nothing	Family and friends are reacting to their like of partner rather than our suitability

Financially rash	6	Major challenge and high risk of financial problems and arguments	Check reactions to my suggestions to finance management strategies	Fear it will result in future arguments over earning and spending priorities
Smoker	5	Partner is considerate about second-hand smoke, but there's a health risk	Partner has tried quitting and failed. It is an irritant, but acceptable	Could become more of an irritant in the future
Lukewarm faith	8	This is a major challenge and crucial to me. A medium chance that partner will become more committed	Raise the question of whether partner will commit more fully. If not, I need to think about our parting, as this is the most important value	I don't want to break up, but my conscience is telling me that I cannot compromise my faith if my partner is going to be half-hearted
Not keen on kids	7	I'm keen on having kids and time's running out	Raise the question with partner again, seeking a definite answer	For me this is an expression of our love and one of the key reasons for marriage

Conclusion: Follow through with suggested actions, but be prepared to suffer the grief of a break-up if I discover our mutual interests are not wide enough, my partner is not really interested in becoming financially responsible, having kids or is unlikely to commit more fully to God.

Because it's easy to select information so that we bias the results, ask God whether there are any pertinent points you might have missed. Remain silent for a few minutes, and then look at the list again. Do any new points come to mind?

In the 'Rank whether it fits your goals and values' column, rate your data in terms of how well each item fits with your key goals and values. If it fits with your main life goals or values, give it a high rating; if it doesn't fit, give it a low rating. So, if working in a Christian environment is important to you and the job you're considering has an anti-religious culture, you would rate it low.

Be realistic and honest. Is your emphasis on bringing home a bigger pay cheque, public recognition and respect, working in a congenial low-stress environment, spending more time with family and friends, serving the community or being an effective witness to God's love? If you're dealing with an ethical question, like whether to report a loved one's illegal drug dealing to the authorities or whether to allow your 17-year-old to have her boyfriend stay with her in her bedroom in your home overnight, your aim might be to do what's best for the other person out of love for them. But you also have your own moral principles and integrity that are important, too. So, list them all.

It can seem like comparing oranges with apples, especially if you're uncertain what your goals and values really are – but try to list them in order, paying particular attention to your long-term and wider objectives and your ethical standards. Avoid being too rigid by thinking in terms of strict moral rules and goals, but instead go for overarching principles. Jesus criticized the religious leaders of his time for being too rule-bound (see, for example, Mark 2.23–28).

Pause and ask God whether the ranking is one that fits with his will. Remain silent again for several minutes before looking again at your rankings and make any necessary adjustments.

Now enter any associated challenges and risks that you can think of in the 'Challenges and risks' column. Note whether you think these are at an excessive, medium or minor level. For example, will insisting that your 17-year-old daughter abide by your values when she's in your home make her want to leave and live with her boyfriend – with the risk that this will produce family disharmony and unhappiness for her later? Or is this an opportunity to learn about relationships and adjust to other people's ethical principles? How do you rate the chances of each? Doing this will help you to have a more detached, objective view of the possibilities.

Pause and ask God whether you have been fair in your assessment and whether you need to modify anything, or if there's anything you need to add. After a short period of silence, review your 'Challenges and risks' column again.

In the 'Actions' column jot down what actions you might need to take for each of the points raised. For many of the points, you may need to do nothing. For some, you may need to seek further information. For others, you may need to come up with ways of handling challenges or lowering risks, while for a few, it'll mean saying yes, no or not now – maybe later.

Your actions could also include a change of attitude. In the case of the 17-year-old, it may mean explaining your stand, saying no to her having the boyfriend stay overnight but taking positive steps to welcome him into the home at other times, and recognizing your daughter's desire for independence and her need to learn from her own relationship decisions. It may also include a resolution to pray for your daughter, her boyfriend and his family.

Take a few moments out to ask God to assess the actions you plan. Listen quietly to him, check the list again and make any changes.

One of the biggest difficulties we face in making decisions is trying to gauge how we really feel about the alternatives. Suppose you're deciding whether to marry the person you're dating (see the table). You might have listed data, such as a strong mutual physical attraction, enjoyment of one another's company, some common interests and the approval of family and friends. These fit in with your values and bode well for your long-term goal of having a happy, successful life together. You might have also noted other traits, such as financial irresponsibility, heavy smoking, lukewarm Christian faith and lack of interest in having children, which are contrary to what you're looking for. How do you go about solving this dilemma?

To help further discern what God might be saying to you, listen to your heart, emotions and conscience. They're important, too. The simplest way to do this is to imagine that you've made your decision to carry out your suggested actions – or, if you're still unsure of what actions to take, imagine each possible action in turn.

In the case of deciding whether to marry, imagine that you've already been married a couple of years, so that the honeymoon experience has faded. Think of what this really implies. Would you enjoy spending time together, pooling financial resources, making decisions and sharing chores? How would you feel about putting off having children for an indeterminate period? Can you make your partner and your home life your first priority? Would you enjoy that or find it irksome? Would it be a fair relationship? Could you trust your partner? Could you imagine your love growing through the good times and bad, in sickness and health until parted by death? Is there a good chance the other person will become a more committed Christian?

Continue to explore your reactions to this imagined situation for a day or two, if time allows. Then try living with the opposite choice. How upset would you be if you went your separate ways? After you got over your initial grief, would you be pleased and feel that your heart and conscience were telling you to find someone more suitable?

Bear in mind that sometimes we might feel uncomfortable or have pangs of conscience about doing the right thing. I felt like this when I first demonstrated against the Vietnam War in the 1960s. That's because I was brought up to believe that Christians should obey those who lawfully govern us and that the way to protest is through the ballot box. But, I also believed New Zealand's involvement in that war was morally wrong and far removed from God's will.

Jot your reactions down in the 'What your heart and conscience say' column.

Now bring all your deliberations back to God in prayer and leave the burden with him (Matt. 11.28). It could help at this stage to seek the counsel of other Christians. If possible, allow several days' breathing space to elapse and then bring your question back to God in prayer and re-examine what you've written in your table.

You may want to make a few changes. Don't expect that your decision will always be a definitive, black-and-white yes or no. As in the marriage example above, God may be directing you to take several other actions first. This could be because God wants to help you come to terms with the inevitable decision you need to make. Or it could be to point you in a different direction.

Be prepared to end up with a very different course of action from any of those you might have outlined. A teacher in my parish was trying to make up her mind over the salary, status and work benefits of several job opportunities when she began to have second thoughts. Something wasn't quite right and her heart kept leading her to focus on what God wanted. She prayed for guidance and, several days later, she had her answer. It came while she was casually flicking through a church magazine. An article on the need for missionary teachers caught her eye and she was soon teaching in a developing country for a fraction of the salary she could have earned.

When we truly open ourselves to God to guide us in our decisions, we open ourselves to unexpected possibilities.

Healing

The foxhole prayers of soldiers under fire show how a major crisis in our lives can bring most of us to our knees. This is especially true when we, or someone we love, are facing tragedy or lying gravely ill. However, over recent years, research into prayer has cast doubts over the effectiveness of prayers for healing. An article entitled 'Faith healing' published on the American Cancer Society website in March 2007 states:

> Available scientific evidence does not support claims that faith healing can cure cancer or any other disease. Even the 'miraculous' cures at the French shrine of Lourdes, after careful study by the Catholic Church, do not outnumber the historical percentage of spontaneous remissions seen among people with cancer. However, faith healing may promote peace of mind, reduce stress, relieve pain and anxiety, and strengthen the will to live.

What are we to make of this? Jesus promised our prayers will be answered. 'If you believe, you will receive whatever you ask for in prayer' (Matt. 21.22).

Although God will always respond to our prayers, we need to be careful not to expect instant miracles. Prayer is not a quick-fix elixir, as if all we have to do is utter a few prayerful formulas, have a bit of faith and presto! – another miracle from God. We can make our requests to him, but God decides what he wants for us. As much as we might like prayer to be an open door to an active, healthy lifestyle, God could have other plans.

The Jews of Jesus' time believed that illness, injury and misfortune were the result of sin. But Jesus was able to show how the hurtful effects of sin are conquered. The miraculous healings described in the New Testament – casting out demons, restoring sight to the blind and hearing to the deaf and the ability to walk to the lame – demonstrate that through Jesus the power of sin can be broken.

The story of the paralytic lowered through the roof of the building where Jesus was preaching illustrates this (Mark 2.1–12). Jesus' first words to the afflicted man were, 'Son, your sins are forgiven.' Some of the Jewish religious leaders regarded this as blasphemous and thought to themselves, 'Who can forgive sins but God alone?' Jesus replied with another question, 'Which is easier: to say to the paralytic, "Your sins are forgiven," or to say, "Get up, take your mat and walk"?' He was making the point that forgiveness of sins is a complex but necessary first step to healing.

The curing of the paralytic is a parable for us all. We need to have faith that God will forgive and that we can be reconciled with him no matter what we have done. Although most of us no longer accept that God punishes us deliberately by inflicting illness or tragedy – these happen by accident, self-neglect and abuse, violence or a quirk of nature – we should still make reconciliation with God our first priority.

Instead of diving headlong into prayer for healing and offering God a list of broken legs, malignant tumours, heart disorders, psychiatric and emotional problems and then sitting back and seeing what kind of answer God will come up with, begin by offering yourself to him.

Because many of us need assurance of God's forgiveness and love, you might prefer to make your confession before a priest or pastor and receive his or her counsel.

Approach God like a child (Matt. 18.3), in total trust and faith. Ask for forgiveness and accept it. By doing this, you are healing your relationship with God and removing the barriers created by your sin. You have now changed the emphasis from what God can do for you to what his will is for you. You are ready to mention your specific petitions and be open to receive the answer. You place yourself at God's disposal and trust him implicitly, rather than pinning your hopes on an instant miracle. Whether or not you or loved ones are cured of a physical ailment is no longer the primary issue.

I remember an English family who made a special pilgrimage to the shrine of Lourdes with their mentally disabled and spastic daughter, Becky. When they returned home, there was no visible improvement in Becky's condition but her parents had changed. 'What we have gained as a family', her mother told me,

> is far more important than having Becky walking and talking like other children, though it would have been lovely if that had happened. Going to Lourdes and being with other Christians in similar circumstances renewed our faith. We gave ourselves to God, just accepting his love instead of expecting a miracle. The wonder of his love comes over you: that is the great miracle.

This story illustrates how often the answer to prayer for healing is not 'take up your bed and walk' but how we may need to live with the illness, and the pain and inconvenience it can cause, especially if there is no cure or satisfactory way of controlling the illness. In offering our predicament to God, we're opening ourselves to his will, knowing that he loves us and stands by us through our ordeal.

My brother, who is now in his mid-fifties, has suffered severe psoriatic arthritis for over 25 years. He had to give up sport and his promising career and cope with periods of immobility and bouts of psoriasis. As part of the grief process, when the symptoms first became serious, he re-evaluated his life, learned to appreciate his family and their love for one another, thought about God and his love and returned to the Church. He has since devoted his life to serving God with an inner sense of peace and contentment that is a witness to others.

The extraordinary will sometimes occur. A cancerous growth shrivels, a terminally ill patient's health improves, the bereaved receive God's consolation and arthritics move their joints without pain. Many who are ill and troubled find that once they surrender to God's love, their own worries and problems seem to diminish. Their trust in God brings about an inner peace. Because prolonged anxiety and stress can have a negative impact on the immune system, this reduction of anxiety will often contribute to a cure. This is particularly true of anxiety, neurosis and stress-related illnesses, such as migraines, back pain and muscle tension, hypertension and heart problems, some types of cancer, arthritis, skin conditions, insomnia and ulcers.

You'll also find that if you're a heavy smoker or drinker, a compulsive overeater, suffer from anorexia or have some other form of addiction, your attitude toward yourself will change once you turn your life over to God. You'll see how your body is, in St Paul's words, 'a temple' in need of proper care (1 Cor. 6.19–20).

In scientific literature, the usual explanation for the positive effects of prayer on illness is that it's caused by a placebo effect. That means that the strong belief in the power of prayer or the abilities of a faith healer helps make the person with the illness feel better. But reducing God to a mere sugar pill or sop belittles the positive impact our faith in God has.

Much of the pain and suffering in our lives comes from broken relationships – death, divorce, shattered romances, splintered families. The death of a loved one is especially hard to bear. As I write this, my elderly mother is near death. There's nothing more I or any of the family can do to help her other than be with her and assure her of God's and our love. Despite our grief at seeing our frail mother gasping for breath, we must accept that 'The LORD gave and the LORD has taken away; may the name of the LORD be praised' (Job 1.21) – especially after a long and fruitful life.

Even so, at times like this we can feel very empty and alone. Our anguish seems insurmountable. In such distressing circumstances it can be difficult to trust in God's love. Yet this is not the time to hide your feelings from him. Pour out all your anger, remorse, resentment and guilt, and ask for his help. Remember that you will not be the only one who's affected; include in your prayers the others who are also suffering.

It can take time to accept God's healing love, but try to remain open to this. You could give thanks for the life of the person who has died and offer to God your memories. You might also want to include in your prayers those who have comforted you during your bereavement.

In another kind of broken relationship, a friend of mine and his sister had a falling-out. It began with a discussion about family finances, but when neither side was prepared to compromise, it degenerated into snide comments and angry reactions. When a situation like this occurs, it's essential to detach yourself from your own point of view and see it from the other person's perspective. Even if you feel that your position is valid, don't attempt to justify it in your own mind. Instead, move away from the immediate situation and ask for God's guidance in helping to understand what happened. When you calm down, review the conflict and try to see how the things you did or said could have hurt the other person.

Perhaps my friend had unwittingly implied that he was superior to his sister since he held a good job while she was unemployed. Try to imagine how you would feel if there were a reversal of roles – if you had to spend the last three months sending out résumés and calling on dozens of firms desperately looking for work and had to swallow your pride and accept a subsidy from your parents.

You might not be able to put yourself in the other person's shoes entirely, but unless you realize how your insensitivity might have contributed to the problem, reconciliation is going to be difficult. It could be helpful to meditate on what Jesus said about not judging others and noticing the speck in someone else's eye while ignoring the plank in your own eye (Matt. 7.1–5). Then ask for God's forgiveness and guidance in effecting reconciliation, and remain in silence allowing him time to speak to you.

When you have done this, you'll be in a better position to approach the other person and maybe to ask him or her for forgiveness or accept an apology – if this is appropriate.

When making contact with the other person after a quarrel, it often helps to sort out the issue that caused the problem if you can start with what you know you have in common. In the case of the brother and sister falling out over finances, what they both agreed on was the importance of sticking to a reduced budget.

Then look at the areas where you are prepared to make a compromise and offer this as a gesture. If it's a question of family finances, maybe you could propose taking public transport instead of the family vehicle to work. This will make the other party more inclined to offer a similar compromise.

Once you've worked through the easy compromises, you can then look at the more difficult issues. My friend's sister was adamant that she needed money for good clothes, as she didn't want to drop her standards and lower her morale. My friend, on the other hand, insisted on going skiing most winter weekends, as this was his passion. At this point, you'll probably each need to trade something to produce a satisfactory compromise. My friend dropped some of his ski trips and his sister agreed to reduce her spending on clothes.

If you can't agree, it may help to invite a mutual friend or Christian pastor acceptable to both, to act as a facilitator and mediator to bring about reconciliation.

Treat your conflict as a positive experience from which you can learn to be more understanding and less judgemental in the future.

In the case of my friend, his sister was so hurt that a year later she still was not happy with the way they were dealing with issues and, at first, she refused to attend his wedding. It might take time to build up trust in each other again. If your efforts fail, don't poison yourself with blame or bear a grudge. Offer the problem to God and leave it with him. Jesus tells us, 'Come to me, all you who are weary and burdened, and I will give you rest' (Matt. 11.28), so why not take his advice?

Sometimes, we can find it impossible to forgive. We feel so badly done by that despite our best efforts to feel otherwise, our anger overwhelms us with a passion for vengeance. I've listened to people who've been sexually assaulted, mugged, burgled, battered, brutalized and swindled. Others who have lost a loved one because of gross negligence or murder have poured out their unhealed emotional wounds and desperate need to seek retribution so they can have emotional closure – whatever that means.

I also felt like this after a burglar I caught in the act of breaking into my car and stealing its contents in a remote part of New Zealand turned on me with a knife. I barely managed to escape and for weeks afterwards, I kept replaying the terror of that knife blade plunging to within a few centimetres of my heart. I couldn't find the 'pause' button to stop the continuous loop in my head. Each time it happened I would adapt the scenario slightly till I'd taken control and disarmed my assailant, beating him until he screamed for mercy. The power of my feelings surprised me. Here was I, a Christian priest, fantasizing about revenge instead of thinking about forgiveness and reconciliation as Jesus did on the cross (Luke 23.34). It didn't help that my attacker, whom I recognized from police photos, had an alibi provided by friends and therefore escaped prosecution for the crime.

Yet, I also knew that my post-traumatic stress feelings were normal for this kind of life-threatening situation. They are part of the burden we bear in these circumstances. What mattered was how I reacted to those feelings. Jesus advises that when a person wrongs us, we should quickly make it up with that person; otherwise get help from others or from members of the church community (Matt. 18.15–20). I did pray for him and talked with leaders in his ethnic community about ways of helping him out of a life of crime. When interviewed on a national radio network, I was able to tell people how I honestly felt, and how with God's help I had to strive to seek forgiveness for him, which was necessary if God was to heal my own emotional pain and the fear the incident had caused.

It may help to seek the help of a trauma counsellor if you're suffering a serious emotional hurt. Bear in mind, though, that constantly talking about a shocking incident may have a negative impact by opening up the wounds and reinforcing in your mind what happened. A good counsellor will know this and help you to overcome your fears and help you readjust. It will take time for the wound to heal. So, after you've prayed for forgiveness for those who've badly hurt you, allow God's love to work slowly through you and don't be ashamed if occasionally you have a flashback that rekindles your anger. Trust that he will help you through the problem with the help and care of others.

In the Epistle of James we are told that if anyone is ill, he should 'call the elders of the church to pray over him and anoint him with oil in the name of the Lord' (Jas. 5.14). Many churches practise the sacrament of anointing, private communion and confession, the laying-on of hands or other types of healing services. If you are in need of any type of healing, you could explore these possibilities through your local church community.

Some faith healers claim they have curative powers. While some people are better at helping us come closer to God and his healing love, there are also many charlatans out there. Check their claims and motives carefully. Is their emphasis on soliciting contributions or putting the spotlight on themselves? Or is it on spreading God's love and salvation as part of a recognized church?

If you think it's a case of demonic possession, you'll need to seek professional assistance from an appropriate psychologist, psychiatrist or pastor. Most clergy are psychologically sensitive and will know when to use the services of an expert exorcist. Fortunately, these occasions are rare.

If you are praying for other people, try to pray with them as this will help reassure them of God's love and that they are part of his caring family. If this is not possible, visualize the people you are praying for or have a picture of them in front of you while you pray. Be ready for the Holy Spirit to lead you into some practical course of action, like helping with chores during a family time of need, bringing flowers or offering valuable companionship and support. You don't have to say much. Just being there is often enough. In these ways, you'll be participating in the healing process.

Whatever the outcome, don't forget to give thanks to God. When Jesus cured the ten lepers (Luke 17.11–19), only one returned to thank him. Don't be like the other nine.

5

MEDITATION AND REFLECTION

Learning to meditate

Whenever my father rose from forty winks on the sofa, he would never admit to having been asleep. He always insisted he'd been meditating. We were supposed to believe he'd been pondering some deep philosophical issue. So, when my father caught me day-dreaming instead of getting on with the job, I would offer him the same explanation. Needless to say, the term 'meditation' became a standard family joke.

But meditation can be productive. It's the practice of taking time out to reflect on a subject, with the aim of discovering worthwhile insights. When used as a prayer method, meditation helps to increase our awareness of God and his will for us.

A number of spiritual writers have given us guidelines as to how to meditate. Some methods such as the rosary, the Stations of the Cross and the Last Words from the Cross, focus on particular events from the Gospels or Church tradition. St Ignatius of Loyola, St Francis de Sales and the Sulpician school provide a structured approach to a topic you choose from the range of topics they suggest. Other forms of meditation have little structure, for instance a simple reflection on nature or a free association. You may choose to meditate on a concrete object such as a seed, a flower, a crucifix, a stained-glass window, a story from the Scriptures or the life of a saint – or more abstract concepts like truth, love, sacrifice or God's mercy.

At the simplest level, a prayer meditation might be a free association. Start with a theological theme and let your mind flow in an uninterrupted stream of consciousness, making whatever connections you like.

If your subject is the second of the Ten Commandments, against worshipping graven images (Exod. 20.4), your associations might flow like this: graven images . . . golden calf . . . Moses on the mountain . . . tablets . . . Ten Commandments . . . Cecil B. DeMille extravaganza . . . lead actor, Charlton Heston . . . romance and sex . . . Hollywood commercialization of God and religion . . . At this point, you might go off on a tangent thinking about the economy, inflation, your own bank account, the bills you need to pay and whether to give less money to your local church or ask for a raise. Our digressions usually lead to what is uppermost in our minds, so treat these detours as an exercise in self-discovery. But don't spend too long on these side excursions. Return to the original topic and begin your associations again. If you do this, you might well view your digressions in a new light. When you reflect on your financial preoccupations in terms of graven images, your associations might now include the ways in which your material goals stand between you and God.

This last technique is a relatively unstructured form of meditation and frequently becomes little more than daydreaming. As a way of helping to avoid this, most meditation techniques give direction and purpose to the meditation. They usually have the following three elements in common: preparation, consideration of the chosen topic, and resolution in which there's a promise to God to carry out a specific action.

Here is an example of simple structured meditation.

Begin by picking a theme: a passage from Scripture, the life of a saint, the words of a well-known prayer, an object from nature, one of the sacraments or a mystery of faith. Think carefully about the topic you choose, making sure you understand it and that it will give you some insights into how you might live a fuller Christian life. If you select Christ's passion – the events from the Last Supper to his execution – and want to go beyond a superficial level, be prepared to allot long periods or break up the subject into instalments.

After your preparation, including informing yourself about the topic and asking for the Holy Spirit's guidance during your meditation (see 'Making contact', pp. 27–30), consider the topic you have decided upon in the light of the questions listed here.

1 What are the facts? What do I know about it? Gather more information from reading, searching the Internet or from others, if you know little about the topic.
2 What does it mean? To me? My relationship with others? My relationship with God?
3 What does God want me to do about it?

Suppose you settle on the topic of baptism. First, think about the facts in terms of what takes place from the standpoint of the candidate, the sponsors or godparents and the congregation. Then consider what it means, especially the symbolism of water. That may remind you of Bible stories like these:

- Israelites escaping from Egypt and crossing the Sea of Reeds to a new life of freedom (Exod. 14).
- Jesus' own baptism, which was the beginning of his ministry (Mark 1.9–11).
- Jesus telling Nicodemus that he needed to undergo a transformation and be born again with water and the Spirit if he was to see the kingdom of God (John 3.1–16).
- Jesus washing his disciples' feet with water and how Peter insisted Jesus clean him all over (John 13.1–15).
- How water and blood flowed when the soldier thrust a spear in Jesus' side (John 19.33–35) showing that he was already dead, but the water was also a sign that his death heralds the birth of the new relationship we can have with God.

Water is also a necessity for life and growth. Without it, most plants and animals die. So, consider what it symbolizes: the cleansing of sin, the breaking of the waters before birth and the association of new life and growth in Christ, the entering of the Holy Spirit and joining a new family, which is the family of God and his Church.

When you reflect on what baptism means to you, recall your own – or, if you were too young to remember, think of the promises made on your behalf. Your thoughts could turn to your own godchildren or the people recently admitted by baptism into your congregation.

What does God want you to do about it? You might want to thank God for the forgiveness and love he has given you and to thank him that you are part of his Church and for all the benefits you have received as a member of the body of Christ. Or maybe your meditation will raise the question of your own commitment to the faith. Perhaps you will consider contacting your godchildren. You might also seek ways to be more welcoming to new members of your parish.

Many recent studies show that what Christians say they believe and pray for has little impact on what they actually do in their lives. In one church where I worked as an assistant priest in Southern California, I remember how the worshippers said 'Amen' to the prayers for peace. Heads nodded when the rector preached about seeking a non-violent solution to the conflict with Libya. Yet at coffee after church, many boasted to me of how America had kicked butt. It was 1986 and in an effort to stop Libyan-sponsored terrorism, US warplanes had just bombed targets in Libya, killing 37 civilians and an untold number of military personnel. It seemed to me that revelling in 'kicking butt' by killing people seemed a strange way for Christians to encourage their government to help answer prayers for peace. If you are going to be serious about your meditations, be prepared to carry out what God really intends you to do, not what you feel like doing. And, try to carry out your intentions as soon as possible. Otherwise, they might end up like so many New Year resolutions.

Most Christian meditations are elaborations on this basic format. For example, in his book with the attention-grabbing title *Eat This Book: A Conversation in the Art of Spiritual Reading*, Eugene H. Peterson (1932–) argues that we don't always read the Bible properly. He says, 'Reading is an immense gift, but only if the words are assimilated, taken into the soul – eaten, chewed, gnawed, received in unhurried delight.' He suggests that we do this through the traditional practice of *lectio divina* or holy reading that provides spiritual insights.

Origen (*c.* 185–254) first mentioned basic *lectio divina* principles around the year 220, which became the basis of monastic meditation. In the twelfth century, Guigo II, a Carthusian monk, wrote *The Ladder of Monks and Twelve Meditations*, which emphasized the four phases or ladder rungs: *lectio, meditatio, oratio* and *contemplatio*. Reading seeks, meditation perceives, prayer asks for, and contemplation tastes the sweetness of mystical union.

Peterson has used a dietary metaphor to explain his version of *lectio divina*. The four steps he recommends are shown in the table below.

Some of the meditation techniques mentioned in this book, such as the time machine, the Salesian devotion and the Spiritual Exercises,

lectio	Bible reading
meditatio	Meditation where you chew and mull over what you've read
oratio	Prayer where you open yourself to respond to God through his Word in the Bible
contemplatio	Contemplation in which what you've read, meditated and prayed becomes absorbed within you so that you live it out

are suitable for an imaginative creation, in all its vividness, of a scene in our minds. The rosary is a controlled means of reflecting on 15 or 20 scenes from the life of Jesus and his mother. The Stations of the Cross enable you to reflect on the 14 traditional sites on the Via Dolorosa or Way of Sorrows that Jesus took from his trial to his death, while the Seven Last Words dwell on the sayings spoken by Jesus on the cross. The close-up is for a detailed examination of a text. As its name suggests, the nature study is concerned with God's creation and the way we treat the environment, as well as objects we've made, whereas the Sulpician approach emphasizes God in the mind, heart and hands.

In much of the literature on spirituality, you'll find the terms meditation and contemplation used interchangeably. To add to the confusion, followers of Asian practices refer to their methods as meditation. Whatever the words used, there's a distinction between the more rational and imaginative discursive process, which I have described here as meditation, and the imageless inner stillness – or resting in God – of the contemplative or mystic.

The time machine

In his famous short novel, *The Time Machine*, H. G. Wells (1866–1946) gives a fictional account of journeys into the fourth dimension. His central character, known only as the Time Traveller, had invented a way of transporting himself into the past or future. Although time travel wasn't an original idea, Wells was the first author to suggest a device for doing it. And ever since his story appeared, the idea of inventing a way to break the time barrier has gripped our imagination and spawned many books, films and TV shows, including the idea of going back in time with our present-day knowledge and trying to change the course of history. Perhaps you've dreamed of meeting Cleopatra, debating with Aristotle, asking Shakespeare whether he wrote *Hamlet*, attending the premiere performance of Handel's *Messiah* or watching the trial and crucifixion of Jesus of Nazareth.

There is some debate among philosophers and scientists as to whether time travel is theoretically possible and, if it were possible, how it would be achieved. Nevertheless, that hasn't dampened our imaginations. In our minds, we can recreate the past or speculate on the future – a useful tool for prayer meditation.

You can imagine yourself as a participant or observer of a scene from the Bible or the lives of the saints. It's like creating a film in your mind: you use your imagination to set the scene, characters and dialogue. Then you imagine yourself as one of the actors in the scene.

You'll need to choose a story that you can visualize. An action scene is best: Jesus driving out the money changers from the temple (Mark 11.15–17), the feeding of the five thousand (Mark 6.30–44), the wedding at Cana (John 2.1–10), the martyrdom of St Stephen (Acts 6.5—8.2), St Paul's shipwreck on Malta (Acts 27.1—28.10) or a parable such as the good Samaritan (Luke 10.29–37).

Once you've decided on a subject, read the passage several times so that you're thoroughly familiar with it. Then select the role you're to play. If you choose to identify with the victim in the narrative of the good Samaritan, imagine yourself on the dusty road winding among the hills between Jerusalem and Jericho. How do you feel? Hot? Tired? What are you thinking? In one of my meditations, this is how I began to picture the scene.

> Heat's stifling. Need to move quickly to get to Jericho before night-fall. Muggers along this track. Plenty of travellers about, though, and it's broad daylight – lowers the risk. Another bend up ahead. Over halfway. About 12 kilometres to go.
>
> 'What the . . .' I gasp. A surge of primeval fear rushes through my body and down my spine. My heart pounds like a team of chariot horses charging into battle. Two men wielding knives leap from behind the rocks. Barefooted, heads and faces covered. Wearing the *thob* shirts and belts embroidered by their womenfolk in the style of Southern Palestine. They aren't Sicarii. Those daggermen only assassinate Romans. These thugs are common thieves and cut-throats.
>
> 'Not a Roman soldier round when you need one,' the cliché flashed through my mind as I turned to escape. Two behind. Trapped. They're pros. One's barely a teenager. A family affair.
>
> 'They're going to kill me. Lord, have mercy.' An inaudible cry of resignation as I wait for the inevitable. A brief shower of stars and blinding lights.
>
> Sun's changed position. Early afternoon. Can't open my eyes. Head's worse than any hangover. Squadrons of irritating flies crawling over my face, up my nose, around my eyes and mouth. Can't brush them away. I'm parched and those opportunistic critters can scramble over me with impunity to suck the moisture from every orifice. Drifting into a stupor again. A crunching sound – a man approaching.

Wearing shoes. Must be well off. He's slowing. Must've seen me. 'Oh God, no.' He'll finish me off. No point, only my soiled loincloth left. He's mumbling the prayer for the dead – needs to stay clean and pure for his holy work. A priest? He's leaving me here. 'Mercy, Lord.' The cry resounds within my pounding head, unable to find its way to my mouth.

Pain's becoming more intense. Beaten me badly. Something's broken . . . Someone else coming . . .

There's no need to be scrupulous about historical accuracy. Does it really matter if you pictured green pastures in this arid region of Palestine, an asphalt road in the first century, or you think, as I did, in terms of thugs who were bands of robbers and murderers who originated in India around the seventeenth century, or kilometres instead of ancient Roman miles and leagues? After all, the purpose of this exercise is to come to a deeper appreciation of the gospel message and its implications for you.

In his Spiritual Exercises, St Ignatius of Loyola (1491–1556) popularized this you-are-there technique (see 'Spiritual Exercises', pp. 120–4). He suggested recreating the scene in our imagination, then considering the main points of the story, what they mean to us and how we can act on them.

What are the most striking points of the story as you visualize it? In the meditation on the good Samaritan, it might be the irony of receiving help from a despised ethnic minority and the hypocrisy of the religious leaders who passed by. Don't forget to include your feelings. Were you angry about being an innocent victim, rejected by those who should have helped and having to accept charity from an outsider? Did you want to hit back at those who attacked you? You mightn't like to admit to such an unchristian sentiment as wanting revenge but most people who've been powerless in the face of an assault desperately want to take back the initiative. Or were you grateful that one person cared?

After you've recalled the main points, spend a few minutes thinking about how they apply to you. With the good Samaritan example, perhaps you could ask yourself these questions:

- What racial prejudices do I have?
- Do I reject other people in need, like the lonely neighbour who wanted to talk with me?

- What about my senile, terminally ill relative in a nursing home?
- Or the itinerants, migrant workers, the under-employed, un-employed, unemployable and others who are regarded by many as being at the bottom of the social ladder?
- Then ask yourself if you really want to befriend or help these people. What have you already done for them and what more could you do?

Once you have thought about how the story relates to you, ask your-self what you intend to do about it: Should I learn more about the customs and culture of the ethnic group about whom I have negative attitudes? Could I help recent immigrants learn my language? When can I invite my neighbour for coffee? Perhaps you could see your ill relative more regularly, lend a hand at a local emergency shelter or offer your experience and talents in some other way. Pray for God's guidance in forming specific resolutions and in carrying them out.

You might care to use the time machine to test the practicality of your resolutions by imagining consequences of these actions. Can you see yourself as a regular visitor to the nursing home? Could you be a close friend to the lonely neighbour, especially if he or she is going to cling to you and rely on you? You might envision yourself per-forming heroic good deeds but, in practice, never carrying out your fine intentions. The aim of the meditation is to encourage you to live the gospel in practical terms, not to become like the H. G. Wells Time Traveller who never returned to the present.

Reflecting on nature

How often have you heard remarks like these: 'I have only to look at a flower, a bird in flight or to think about the intricacies of the human body to know that God is around me and within me'; 'I feel at one with God as I hike through the wilderness and the country-side'? Perhaps you've uttered them yourself. You may also have heard people say, 'I come closer to God hitting a ball around the golf course or while fishing than I do in church or on my knees praying.'

Some of these attitudes are little more than an excuse for preferring the outdoors. They can also reflect a naturalistic pantheistic view – that God is nature – rather than nature being the creation of God the Creator, the first person of the Trinity. In other words, we can make the mistake of worshipping the creation rather than the Creator.

And, then, there are those who point to the popular example of St Francis of Assisi (1181–1226), patron saint of animals and the environment. He certainly appreciated how we are interconnected with nature and he wrote how God's creation should praise the Creator and inspire us to greater love and respect for our world. His *Canticle of the Sun* is his best-known prayer-hymn.

> We praise You, Lord, for all your creatures,
> especially for Brother Sun,
> who is the day through whom you give us light.
> And he is beautiful and radiant with great splendour,
> of you Most High, he bears your likeness. (second verse)

Even so, many of St Francis' environmental attitudes were common for the thirteenth century and, alas, most of the stories of his special relationship with animals are pure myth.

Nevertheless, when we pause to reflect on nature – the ocean's immensity and changing moods, the vastness of the galaxies, the miracle of new life, or even the ecological role of the mosquito – we can feel awe and praise for God. We can also become concerned at the damage we do to the environment. This fascination with nature and our alarm over the future of the planet can be the basis of a meditation, which can lead to an awareness of God's presence and our place in his creation.

Choose an object you know something about and can examine in detail: a leaf, flower, feather, shell, rock, vegetable, fruit or seed. You might also want to consider a pet or another animal. Observe it closely. Shut your eyes and touch your chosen object. Is it rough or smooth, hard or soft, rigid or pliable? Does it have a smell or make sounds? Now open your eyes and take a good look at it from different angles. What shape and colours does it have? What are its component parts and how do they fit together? Learn as much as you can about the object from your own senses before considering its significance and the symbolic associations it might evoke.

If you decide to meditate on a stalk of wheat, feel the kernels, noting the texture, firmness, colour and shape. Split one or two of them and look at the grains inside. When you've made your observations, turn your attention to its various functions. What part does it play in the ecological chain? Does it provide food or contribute to the nitrogen or carbon cycles? What effect does human involvement have?

In the case of the wheat, it's both food and seed. It's also grown and harvested by humans, using processes that might have a negative impact on other parts of the environment. After you've gained an appreciation of its place in the natural order and of our interaction with it, thank God for his creation and ask for direction in using wisely all he has given us.

This could lead you to think of your role as a steward for the environment. Maybe you'll want to reconsider the kind of food you eat, packaging and recycling, air travel, the use of your motor vehicle and whether to buy a more fuel-efficient model. You might also want to plant more trees, exchange incandescent light bulbs for ones that are more efficient and to use other eco-friendly gadgets, put on more warm clothes, lower the thermostat and use more effective insulation in your home. But the Holy Spirit could lead you in other directions.

The next step is to consider possible symbolic associations. In the parable of the sower (Mark 4.3–20), Jesus provides an illustration of an analogy drawn from nature. The seed symbolizes the word and the seeds that grow to maturity represent those of us who hear the word and act on it, some of us producing better results than others. The seed that falls by the wayside grows for a bit then withers or is choked by weeds, standing for those of us who don't remain true. Perhaps you'll find a lesson like this in nature. According to legend, St Patrick (dates unknown) in the fifth century reflected on a three-leaf clover, or shamrock, and then used it as an aid to teach the Irish about the Trinity – three equal divine persons in one God.

A rock might bring to mind St Peter, whose name in Greek means 'rock' and on whom Jesus said he was building his Church (Matt. 16.18–19). The meditation on the wheat could raise thoughts about 'Give us this day our daily bread' from the Lord's Prayer (Matt. 6.9–13), how Jesus said, 'I am the living bread' (John 6.51) and the Eucharist (Luke 22.19–20; 1 Cor. 10.16–17; 11.23–25).

A meditation on a blowfly or mosquito will probably get you thinking of how these buzzing nuisances that get bad press for spreading disease are an instrument of evil and the animal equivalents of Nazi SS troops. Should our meditations then make us more willing to accept these pests as a special gift from God?

True, they are part of God's creation, yet the ill effects of blowflies, mosquitoes, rats and those malicious bacteria that lay us low are no different from the misery we humans can create. That could inspire you to think of wars and conflicts, illness and death through injustice, poverty and greed, as well as our destruction of the environment – and what you can do about it, including how you can add these issues to your more regular prayers.

In a meditation class I led many years ago, a recently divorced man who fixed his attention on a leaf felt that the difference between its rough and smooth sides could be a comment on his attitude to life. Up to then he had focused on the rough side – domestic turmoil and the trauma of separation – to the exclusion of the positive or smooth side of his life: his children, close supportive friends, good health, a rewarding career and the love of God. In the same class, a teenager concentrating on a dandelion at first related the plainness of the flower to her own lack of beauty and confidence. After looking more closely, she started to realize that, like the flower with its many petals, she possessed many talents and special qualities, and as it was a cheerful yellow colour, she, too, could be cheerful about her own unique God-given attributes.

Pray that the Holy Spirit will show you what you can learn from nature. But don't force tenuous or bizarre associations – the symbolism could become far-fetched. If nothing figurative comes to mind, just appreciate God's creation and give praise and thanks – as the psalmist does in the song of praise (Ps. 148).

Sometimes the object itself will suggest a course of action. After examining the wheat and thinking of it as a basic source of food, an image might flash through your mind of the hungry and deprived who make up the majority of the world's population, and this could lead you to investigate what contribution you can make. A meditation on a pine cone might prompt you to see what you can do to prevent the destruction of forests, including joining a conservation group and planting trees.

When I planted some shrubs and trees in my own home after a nature meditation, I was delighted to see my closest neighbours soon follow my example. Other neighbours did the same and tree plantings became a popular neighbourhood activity. I learned from that never to underestimate the power of God working through what you might think are small and insignificant actions. I should have remembered the parable Jesus told of how the mustard seed is tiny, yet it produces the largest of garden plants that grows into a tree (Matt. 13.31–32).

At other times, your course of action will depend on the symbolic associations you make. In my meditation class, the man who saw a parallel with his divorce when he looked at the rough and smooth sides of the leaf resolved to thank God for the good things that happened each day. The resolution of the teenager who looked on herself as a Plain Jane, on the other hand, was to make a note of three positive qualities every day for a week, to thank God for them and ask him how she could strengthen those good qualities and use them in his service.

You can extend this meditation method to include tools, machinery, buildings and other inanimate objects. The procedure is the same. A hoe or a rake could lead you to thoughts about weeding a garden and, by extension, to cultivating your spiritual life. A machine might impress you with the intricacy of its design and move you to reflect on the complexity of human beings and God's design for us, while a church building might raise questions about your involvement with the Christian community and the active part you could play as a member of God's family.

The close-up

'I need time for it all to sink in,' first-time visitors have remarked after a church service. It's a comment that those of us who attend regularly could take to heart, especially when it comes to familiar prayers like the Lord's Prayer, *Gloria in Excelsis Deo* (Glory to God in the highest), *Anima Christi* (Soul of Christ, sanctify me), *Ave Maria* (Hail Mary) and the *Magnificat* (Song of Mary, Luke 1.46–55), which are repeated regularly.

In the same way that a photographer helps us appreciate the overview of a scene by focusing on the close-ups, we can come to a fuller understanding of these prayers when we examine them in detail word by word or a phrase at a time.

Begin by selecting a prayer, the creeds, parts of the liturgy or scriptural passages like the eight beatitudes from Jesus' sermon on the mount (Matt. 5.3–12; see also Luke 6.20–23) and the Ten Commandments (Exod. 20.1–17; Deut. 5.6–21).

After you have chosen a text, say it through several times, so that you're familiar with it as a whole.

Then break it down into manageable segments. Most prayers, like the Peace Prayer, which is wrongly attributed to St Francis, lend themselves to a phrase-by-phrase analysis, while you can view the Jesus Prayer or the Lord's Prayer microscopically a word or two at a time.

Start with the first word or phrase. Let the associations flow. Then move on to the second word or phrase. One woman reported to me that she had never before appreciated the first word of the Lord's Prayer until she began to meditate on the implications of the 'our' of 'Our Father'. 'It brought home to me', she said, 'that this was not just *my* Father, but *our* Father. Until then, I'd been treating him as though I was an only child.'

This single word was enough to occupy her meditation. When St Ignatius recommended this technique in his Spiritual Exercises, he advised the person meditating to reflect on a word 'as long as he finds meanings, comparisons, relish and consolation in considerations pertaining to such word'.

The popular Peace Prayer first appeared anonymously as *une belle prière à faire pendant la messe* (a beautiful prayer to say during the Mass) in the French spiritual magazine *La Clochette* (*The Little Bell*) in December 1912. It became associated with St Francis of Assisi when it appeared eight years later as the *Prayer of Peace* on the back of a card bearing an image of the saint.

> Lord, make me an instrument of your peace.
> Where there is hatred, let me sow love;
> where there is injury, pardon;
> where there is doubt, faith;
> where there is despair, hope;
> where there is darkness, light;
> where there is sadness, joy.
>
> O Divine Master, grant that I may seek not so much to be consoled
>   as to console;
> to be understood as to understand;
> to be loved as to love;
> for it is in giving that we receive;
> it is in pardoning that we are pardoned;
> and it is in dying that we are born to eternal life. Amen.

As you review each phrase, you could think of instances of hatred, injury and doubt on a global or local level and practical ways to extend love, offer pardon or increase faith. Don't feel you must complete meditating on the whole prayer in one session. You might prefer to spread your meditations over several days or weeks. The next time you return to the prayer, begin by repeating it over in its entirety before resuming your meditation.

The rosary

The rosary is the most popular of all meditation techniques – especially among Roman Catholics. And, although many Protestants have shied away from the rosary because of its emphasis on Mary, some have recognized the value of the rosary as a disciplined form of meditation and have adapted it.

In his Apostolic Exhortation *Marialis Cultus*, Pope Paul VI (1897–1978) described it:

> As a Gospel prayer centred on the mystery of the redemptive incarnation, the Rosary is a prayer with a clear Christological orientation. Its characteristic element, the litany-like succession of Hail Marys, becomes in itself an increasing prayer to Christ who is the ultimate object both of the Angel's announcement, and the greeting by Elizabeth, the Mother of the Baptist – 'the blessed fruit of your womb'. (Luke 1.42)

Pope Pius XII (1876–1958) called the rosary 'the compendium of the entire gospel' and influential Victorian theologian John Cardinal Newman (1801–90) preached a short sermon to the boys at Oscott College in the north of Birmingham in October 1879, in which he said:

> Now the great power of the Rosary lies in this, that it makes the Creed into a prayer; of course, the Creed is in some sense a prayer and a great act of homage to God; but the Rosary gives us the great truths of His life and death to meditate upon, and brings them nearer to our hearts.

The rosary, which highlights the main events in the life of Jesus and his mother, is a pocket-size way of turning the gospel and the creed into prayer. It acts as an intercession, meditation, and reminder of the essentials of our Christian faith.

This devotion originally grew out of the early monastic practice of reciting the 150 psalms as part of the divine office. While some of the monks knew them all by heart and a few could read them, the rest had to substitute an equivalent number of rote prayers, usually the Jesus Prayer (see 'The Jesus Prayer', pp. 146–50), 150 'Our Fathers' or 'Hail Marys' – a custom also adopted by the laity. This earned it the label 'The People's Psalter'. Since it was easy to lose count of the prayers, knotted ropes, beads and other devices came into use.

Interestingly, the word 'bead' comes from 'bede', which in Middle English (1066–1500) meant a prayer. 'Seien bedes' meant reciting prayers and 'peir bedes' referred to rosary beads.

The rosary gradually evolved from a simple recitation of rote prayers to a more complex combination of meditation and memorized prayer. Although the name of St Dominic (1170–1221) is associated with the rosary, it wasn't until the sixteenth century that the rosary took its modern form.

Unlike many other meditation methods, which leave the choice of subject matter open to those doing the meditation, the traditional rosary consists of 15 prescribed scenes from the Gospel stories of the life of Jesus, his mother, Mary, and the early Church receiving the Holy Spirit. These scenes or mysteries, as they are called, are in three clusters of five meditations. The first five, known as the Joyful Mysteries, comprise:

1 *Annunciation* The Angel Gabriel announces to the Virgin Mary that she will bear a son to be named Jesus (Luke 1.26–38).
2 *Visitation* The pregnant Mary visits her cousin Elizabeth before Elizabeth gives birth to John the Baptist (Luke 1.39–56).
3 *Nativity* Jesus is born in Bethlehem (Luke 2.1–16; Matt. 1.18–25).
4 *Presentation* Mary goes to the temple for purification and, as Jesus is the first-born male, he is consecrated to God as someone who belongs to God or is a son of God (Luke 2.21–38; see also Exod. 13.1–14).
5 *Finding Jesus in the temple* The 12-year-old Jesus astounds teachers and experts in Hebrew law at the temple (Luke 2.41–52).

The second group of mysteries, called the Sorrowful Mysteries, focuses on Jesus' passion and death.

6 *Agony in the Garden of Gethsemane* Jesus sweats and prays in trepidation as he submits to his Father's will (Mark 14.32–51).
7 *Scourging at the pillar* The whipping of Jesus with the Roman *flagellum*, which had flesh-tearing bone or metal at the tips (John 19.1–3).

8 *Crowning with thorns* The Roman garrison mocks Jesus' claims to kingship (Matt. 27.27–31).

9 *Carrying the cross* Jesus struggles to make his way to Golgotha (Matt. 27.31–33).

10 *Crucifixion* Jesus dies on the cross for our sins (Matt. 27.34–56; Luke 23.32–49; John 19.18–37).

The last group, the Glorious Mysteries, consist of:

11 *Resurrection* Jesus rises from the dead and his followers find his body gone from the tomb (Matt. 28.1–15; Mark 16.1–8; Luke 24.1–12; John 20.1–29).

12 *Ascension* Jesus goes to be with his Father 40 days after his resurrection (Mark 16.19; Acts 1.1–10).

13 *Descent of the Holy Spirit* At Pentecost, 50 days after the resurrection, the disciples receive the Holy Spirit (Acts 2.1–4).

14 *Assumption* Heaven receives Mary (Rev. 12.1–17).

15 *Coronation* Mary is crowned Queen of Heaven.

In 2002, Pope John Paul II in his apostolic letter *Rosarium Virginis Mariae* suggested adding another five mysteries, which he called the Luminous Mysteries – Mysteries of Light. These are:

16 *Baptism of Jesus* John the Baptist baptizes Jesus, which is the means for God to recognize Jesus and is the beginning of his public ministry (Mark 1.9–11; John 1.29–34).

17 *Wedding at Cana* At the request of his mother, Jesus turns water into good quality wine (John 2.1–11).

18 *Jesus proclaims the kingdom of God* Jesus frequently mentions the kingdom of God, which he describes as here already, within us and to come. The parable of the sower (Mark 4.3–20) and how he tells Nicodemus that we must be born again (John 3.1–21) if we are to experience the kingdom of God are good examples of Jesus' teachings on the kingdom.

19 *Transfiguration* Jesus appears in radiant white clothes talking with the ancient Hebrew prophets, Moses and Elijah, who were said to have been taken bodily into heaven (Mark 9.2–13).

20 *Institution of the Eucharist* At the Last Supper, Jesus referred to how the bread he broke and the wine they drank was his body and blood given to his disciples and all who continue to follow him (Luke 22.19–20; 1 Cor. 11.23–25).

It is customary to pray only one set of five mysteries at a time. Unless your rosary is an oversize model, you'll have to go around three times to pray all 15 mysteries, or four times if you add the Mysteries of Light.

You can meditate on these mysteries in any number of ways. You might imagine the scene from the standpoint of Jesus, his mother or yourself as an observer (see 'The time machine', pp. 81–4). Alternatively, you could linger on one particular aspect of the mystery, such as joy at the coming of Jesus, the poverty and humility of his birth in the manger or his obedience in suffering and dying on the cross. Or you may draw some practical resolution from the meditation like the need to be prepared to take up your cross daily and be true to the faith whatever the cost.

However you focus on the mysteries, your meditation should occupy the foreground while your verbal prayers – the Lord's Prayer, Hail Mary and *Gloria Patri* – said silently or aloud, remain in the background.

At first, it will seem like trying to rub your stomach and pat your head at the same time but, after practice, the verbal prayers will become automatic and remain in the background while you focus on your meditation.

You say the Hail Mary this way:

> Hail Mary, full of grace,
> the Lord is with you;
> blessed are you among women
> and blessed is the fruit of your womb, Jesus.
> Holy Mary, Mother of God,
> pray for us sinners;
> now and at the hour of our death. Amen.

The *Gloria Patri* or 'Glory be' as it is sometimes called, usually takes this form:

> Glory be to the Father and to the Son and to the Holy Spirit.
> As it was in the beginning, is now and ever shall be,
> world without end. Amen.

You don't need beads to pray the rosary, but it frees your mind for the meditations if you have a means of keeping track of the vocal prayers. Most rosaries have five sets of ten Hail Mary beads with a single Our Father bead in between. These beads are in a circle and constitute the main body of the rosary. An appendage, which

Hail Mary 10 x
Lord's Prayer
Second Mystery
Gloria Patri
Hail Mary 10 x

Gloria Patri
Lord's Prayer
Third Mystery

Lord's Prayer
First Mystery
Your petitions
Gloria Patri

Hail Mary 3 x

Hail Mary 10 x
Hail Mary 10 x

Lord's Prayer

Gloria Patri
Lord's Prayer
Fifth Mystery
Lord's Prayer
Fourth Mystery

Gloria Patri
Apostles' Creed

Hail Mary 10 x

Rosary

includes the crucifix and five additional beads, is for preparatory prayers (see the figure above).

To pray the rosary, begin at the crucifix and repeat the Apostles' Creed:

> I believe in God the Father Almighty, creator of heaven and earth:
> and in Jesus Christ his only Son, our Lord,
> who was conceived by the Holy Spirit,
> born of the Virgin Mary,
> suffered under Pontius Pilate,
> was crucified, died and was buried;
> he descended to the dead.
> On the third day he rose again;
> he ascended into heaven,
> and sits at the right hand of God the Father Almighty;
> from there he shall come to judge the living and the dead.
> I believe in the Holy Spirit; the holy Catholic Church,
> The communion of saints,
> the forgiveness of sins,
> the resurrection of the body,
> and the life everlasting. Amen.

Now proceed to the first bead and say the Lord's Prayer (see 'What to say', pp. 31–5). On the next three beads – which, according to different traditions, symbolize the Holy Trinity or faith, hope and charity – pray three Hail Marys and follow this with the *Gloria Patri*.

At this point, you might prefer to insert your special petitions to God before moving on to the mysteries.

After you've made your requests, announce the first mystery and describe it to yourself in a few words.

While you meditate on its meaning, repeat the Lord's Prayer on the fifth bead – the first of the five large or detached beads. Continue your reflections as you pray Hail Mary ten times counting through the next ten beads and finishing the decade with the *Gloria Patri*.

Then announce the second mystery and say the Lord's Prayer on the next Our Father bead. Continue the same procedure through-out the rest of the rosary (see figure of a rosary).

Many people pray the Fatima Prayer on each of the large or detached beads as well as the Lord's Prayer and the *Gloria Patri*. The Fatima Prayer is a result of the apparition of Mary that appeared first to three shepherd children and then to others at Fatima in Portugal in 1917. This short prayer has similarities with the Jesus Prayer (see 'Jesus Prayer', p. 148).

> O my Jesus, forgive us our sins, save us from the fires of hell, lead all souls to heaven, especially those in most need of your mercy. Amen.

When praying the rosary aloud in a group, it is customary to add Marian prayers, such as *Salve Regina* (Hail, Holy Queen) or the *Memorare* (Remember, O Most Gracious Virgin Mary) at the con-clusion of the five decades or one set of mysteries. It is also normal, especially when praying the rosary on your own, to end with a thanks-giving to God.

Although the rosary is a structured meditation, there is room for flexibility. Sometimes you may wish to pray the rosary by con-centrating on only one or two mysteries instead of five. At other times, you may want to meditate on the verbal prayers rather than the mysteries or you may find yourself drawn into affective contem-plation, where you linger in God's presence. If you find it difficult to meditate and recite vocal prayers simultaneously, you can always say these prayers after you've meditated on the mystery.

While the Dominican rosary is the most common, there are many others. Some are variations, like the seven-decade Franciscan crown, which extends the number of joyful mysteries to include the

Magi or wise men visiting the infant Jesus (Matt. 2.1–12); the chap-
let of St Joseph, which retains all 15 traditional mysteries, but has
fewer verbal prayers; or the Birgittine rosary, which has six decades,
seven Our Fathers and 63 Hail Marys. Other rosaries emphasize
particular themes such as the special sorrows of Our Lady, the 13
virtues of St Anthony, the Holy Spirit, the Sacred Heart of Jesus, the
Blessed Sacrament or the Stations of the Cross (see 'Stations of the
Cross', pp. 97–112). Simple single-decade rosaries are also popular,
while Christians in the Eastern Orthodox tradition may use a prayer
rope while saying the Jesus Prayer (See 'Jesus Prayer', p. 148).

Of the societies that promote the rosary, the Confraternity of the
Holy Rosary, the Legion of Mary and the Rosary League are active
within the Roman Catholic Church, whereas the Living Rosary of
Our Lady and St Dominic encourages the practice among Anglicans.

One way in which Protestants have adapted the rosary is to
reduce the number of mysteries to a basic five: the nativity, agony
in the garden, crucifixion, resurrection and the descent of the Holy
Spirit at Pentecost. You could also include the Luminous Mysteries
along with other scriptural material – Jesus' temptations in the
wilderness (Matt. 4.1–11), recruiting of the disciples (Matt. 4.18–22),
the triumphant entry into Jerusalem (Mark 11.1–11), the Last
Supper (Mark 14.12–26) and the Seven Last Words from the cross
(Luke 23.34, 43; John 19.26–27; Mark 15.34; John 19.28, 30; Luke
23.46). Alternative verbal prayers could include the Jesus Prayer or
the *Sanctus*:

> Holy, holy, holy, Lord God of power and might,
> heaven and earth are full of your glory.
> Glory be to you, O Lord most high.

Another possibility is verse 14 from Psalm 19: 'May the words of my
mouth and the meditation of my heart be pleasing in your sight,
O Lord, my Rock and my Redeemer.'

There are numerous possibilities.

Rosary beads have been fashioned of precious stones and metal
like gold and silver, as well as wood, ivory, rose petals and olive pips.
You don't have to use commercially made beads. You could make your
own. A knotted string, handkerchief or some other counting device –
even your ten fingers – can serve as a tactile aid to make your meditations more systematic and your prayer life more ordered.

Stations of the Cross

The Stations of the Cross is a meditation on a series of 14 scenes during the final hours and death of Jesus. Sometimes called Via Crucis (the Way of the Cross), Via Dolorosa (Way of Sorrows) or merely the Way, it is second only to the rosary in popularity – particularly among Roman Catholics, Anglicans, Lutherans and some in the Eastern Orthodox Church, especially during Lent, Holy Week and Good Friday.

You can meditate on the stations privately, in groups or as part of a church service.

This form of meditation arose among the many pilgrims who visited sites in the Holy Land, especially from the time of Emperor Constantine in the early fourth century when chapels began to appear at holy sites, and then the further influx of European visitors after the Crusaders captured Jerusalem from Muslims in the twelfth century. Pilgrims would visit places like Bethlehem, the Jordan River, the Sea of Galilee, the road to Jericho and, of course, all the holy sites in Jerusalem, especially the traditional places celebrated since the second century as sites where Jesus underwent the passion of his final hours.

At each place, or station, where a special event may have occurred, pilgrims meditated on what happened to Jesus and offered prayers and devotions. Some re-enacted what they believed happened to Jesus at each station, starting with the place of his death sentence and then along the several hundred-metre journey to the execution site. Even today, a few Christians take Jesus' call to take up their cross and follow him (Mark 8.34) in a literal way by carrying a wooden cross through the streets of Jerusalem on Good Friday.

For most that couldn't make the trip to the Holy Land, the practice grew in Europe of creating scenes and shrines that replicated what happened to Jesus at these special stations. That enabled the faithful to make a spiritual rather than a physical pilgrimage. St Jerome (*c.*347–419) even argued in his letter to Paulinus, written about 395, that going to the Holy Land wasn't important, as 'access to the courts of heaven is as easy from Britain as it is from Jerusalem; for "the kingdom of God is within you"'.

At first the number and type of stations varied, including stations like: Jesus tastes the gall (Matt. 27.34), Judas betrays Jesus (Mark

14.43–46), Jesus is flogged (John 19.1) or crowned with thorns (John 19.2–3). Some pilgrims also made devotions at places like the Jerusalem Gate and the Ecce Homo Arch. It wasn't until the end of the seventeenth century that there began to be common agreement on the 14 stations. They reflect ancient tradition as well as accounts recorded in the Gospels.

A criticism of some meditations on the Stations of the Cross is that they romanticize Jesus' suffering and dwell on incidents that are from legend rather than the Gospels. The explanation and suggested meditations that I have given for each of the 14 stations in the table on pp. 99–105 take into account these criticisms.

Although you need only meditate on the 14 stations, it is normal to begin and end your meditations with prayer and to pray before and after each station. There are plenty of possible prayers to choose from. Below are some suggestions:

- *Opening prayer*

> Lord Jesus Christ,
> take me along the path
> you once took to your death.
> Take all that I am,
> my thoughts, my imagination, my memory,
> my heart, feelings, my will and all my weaknesses
> and show me what you did
> out of love for me and all the world.
> Cleanse me of sin and teach me how to follow your example.
>   Amen.

- *Before each station*

> We adore you, O Christ, and we bless you,
> because by your holy cross,
> you have redeemed the world.

- *After each station*

> Lord, you remained obedient unto death for us, even death on the cross.
> Thank you, Lord, for this meditation. Show me how best to serve you, now and always.

The Lord's Prayer; Hail Mary; *Gloria Patri* (Glory be).

(*continued on p. 106*)

1 *Jesus is condemned to death*	After he's accused by the High Priest Caiaphas of blasphemy and mocked by Herod, Jesus appears before the Roman Governor Pontius Pilate. Whether this happened at the traditional site of Madrasa al-Omariya or at Herod's palace near the Jaffa Gate is a matter of debate. Pilate, believing Jesus innocent of sedition against Rome, gives the people the choice of freeing Jesus or Barabbas. They choose Barabbas and demand Pilate crucify Jesus. After symbolically washing his hands of any blame, Pilate condemns Jesus to die after he's flogged and mocked as a pretend king and made to wear a crown of thorns. Some scholars believe flogging Jesus was an act of mercy on Pilate's part (Matt. 27.11–26; John 19.1–16); he may have thought it would appease the crowd, thus enabling him to release Jesus, or that it would hasten Jesus' death if the crowd wanted him crucified.	Imagine the ordeal that Jesus underwent – forsaken by disciples who promised to stand by him, falsely accused, misunderstood, mocked, severely beaten and condemned to an appalling death because of popular demand from the very people he'd come to save. Yet, he remained steadfast and faithful to his calling.

Think of ways in which you belittle and condemn others through malicious gossip or how you might summarily dismiss them as irrelevant. Give thanks for Jesus' steadfast faithfulness under extreme provocation. Pray also for those who reject Christ as saviour. |
| 2 *Jesus receives the cross* | Suffering the psychological ordeal of his trial and mockery as well as the trauma of scourging by a flesh-tearing barbed whip, Jesus begins the journey to Golgotha, Calvary or Place of the Skull, where his execution will occur. It was customary for the condemned to carry the | Envision Jesus receiving the extra burden of the crossbar. Also remember how he tells his disciples that he expects those who follow him to take up their cross daily and be prepared to lose their lives for his sake and that of the gospel (Mark 8.34–38). |

crossbar of their cross to the site of execution, which is probably what Jesus did (John 19.17).

3 Jesus falls the first time

Exhausted and suffering from pain and hypovolemic shock due to loss of blood, Jesus falls under the weight of the crossbar.

4 Jesus meets his mother

Tradition suggests that Mary met her scourged and condemned son on the way to his execution and fainted. Writings from the fourth century also mention how Mary revisited the sites of Jesus' last hours and prayed at those places.

Consider ways in which you let Jesus down by not wanting to stand out, through feeling embarrassed and awkward about your faith or putting other goals like your welfare, career, status, success and money first.

Remember how Jesus told those who are weary and burdened to learn from him. He promises that through following him, we will find inner peace and rest for our souls (Matt. 11.28–29).

Pray that God will give you the strength to carry any extra burdens laid on you with which you're having difficulty coping. Ask that you will find inner joy and peace of mind.

Despite our adoration of Mary and her concern for her son, the Gospels tell us that Jesus instructed his supporters to forsake their families for his sake. He said those who followed him and did God's will were his mother, brother and sister (Mark 3.31–34). He also reminded followers that the cost of discipleship could mean hating your own family, including your spouse, children or even your own life (Luke 14.25–27).

5 Simon of Cyrene helps carry the cross

As Jesus becomes unable to carry his own crosspiece, the crucifixion squad order Simon from Cyrene (a community of Cyrenian ex-patriots within Palestine rather than Cyrene in Libya) to shoulder the burden. St Mark's Gospel tells us Simon was visiting Jerusalem from the country and was the father of Alexander and Rufus (Mark 15.21).

Pray for your own family and consider whether you put family and others ahead of following Jesus, and ask for God's guidance.

Think about the things that burden others and how you might help shoulder some of their problems to help free them.

Pray that God will guide you and give you the energy to do this willingly and joyfully.

6 Veronica wipes Jesus' face

A legend that became popular in the Middle Ages suggests that a pious woman of Jerusalem took pity on Jesus and wiped the tears and blood from his face with her veil, leaving an imprint that became an object of veneration. Veronica is occasionally associated with Martha of Bethany (John 11.1–44) or the woman with the haemorrhage who touched Jesus' robe (Matt. 9.20). However, there is no evidence that a Veronica or any other woman wiped Jesus' face.

The story of Veronica is of someone moved to do a small act of compassion when others have forsaken Jesus.

It's worth deliberating on what opportunities you have to offer small acts of kindness to others.

Ask God for his help to act on these opportunities. In the parable of the sheep and the goats (Matt. 25.31–46), Jesus reminds his listeners that whenever we offer compassion we also do it for him.

7 Jesus falls a second time

Despite Simon carrying the crossbar, which enables Jesus to stagger on ahead unencumbered (Luke 23.26), Jesus is so weak he stumbles again.

Meditate on how Jesus goes to his death bearing our sins (Gal. 1.3–5).

Think of what separates you from God, what mistakes you have made and the many missed opportunities to help spread his kingdom of love.

8 Jesus meets women of Jerusalem

Many people follow Jesus, especially women from Jerusalem who act like professional mourners, weeping and wailing his imminent death. Jesus reprimands them, urging them to weep for themselves, not for him, as the time will soon come when they wished they had no children (Luke 23.27–31). Many see this warning as a reference to the Great Jewish Revolt between 66 and 73 AD that resulted in the Romans destroying Jerusalem in 70 AD.

Because Jesus' execution was necessary to bring in the new covenant of God's forgiving love, mourning his imminent demise seems inappropriate. We are reminded of how Jesus likened Peter to Satan when he tried to dissuade him from taking the path which led to death (Mark 8.31–33).

Instead, we should think of others who suffer, especially those persecuted for the faith and those who persecute them.

9 Jesus falls a third time

In a weakened state through loss of blood, shock and pain, Jesus collapses again and is forced to continue the remaining few metres to Golgotha, just outside the first-century wall of Jerusalem – probably at the sacred site now within the Church of the Holy Sepulchre.

Jesus' third fall is a reminder that we too continue to fall through bad habits and frequent lapses of unloving and selfish behaviour and that Jesus continues to bear our mistakes and love us. When Peter asked Jesus how many times we should forgive, Jesus replied that it wasn't seven times, but 77 times (Matt. 18.21–22).

Give thanks that Jesus continues to bear our sins and love us.

10 *Jesus is stripped*

When the execution party arrives at Golgotha, the soldiers strip Jesus stark naked of all his blood-soaked garments. At this time, garments were all handwoven and in demand. As a side-benefit of their gruesome task, the soldiers divide Jesus' clothes between the four of them and cast lots for his seamless undergarment (John 19.23–24).

Similar to the way in which Jesus is born as a homeless outcast, he goes to his death naked and humiliated as an outcast.

Ponder the ways in which you have false shame, pride, conceit, and seek status and recognition.

Ask God for the humility and strength to be obedient to him and to have pride in serving him alone.

11 *Crucifixion: Jesus is nailed to the cross*

Jesus suffers the ignominy, pain and the horrendous physical stress of crucifixion with two other offenders, who must have been guilty of crimes against Roman rule to suffer crucifixion. Pilate orders a sign stating 'Jesus of Nazareth, the King of the Jews' placed on Jesus' cross. And, although many mock him, Jesus forgives them and his executioners and tells the offender alongside him who asks to be remembered, that today he joins him in paradise (John 19.19–22; Luke 23.33–43).

It can be very hard to forgive those who really hurt us, especially those who profess love and then cheat on us or forsake us, as well as those who damage our career, financial prospects or those we love.

Bring before God those you try to forgive, but against whom you still harbour a grudge deep down. Recall how Jesus told us to put things right with those we fall out with and that in the Lord's Prayer we pray that we be forgiven our sins as we forgive others.

12 Jesus dies on the cross

Those crucified had difficulty breathing with arms outstretched and lungs extended. They eventually died from asphyxiation, which could take several days or a few hours, depending on the physical state of the victim. So that Jesus and the other two victims could die and their bodies be buried before the Jewish Sabbath, Pilate orders their legs broken. This would make it harder for victims to breathe, causing death within a few hours. Loss of blood and the trauma of the flogging hastened Jesus' death, so there was no need to break his legs. Before he dies, Jesus wonders whether God has forsaken him, arranges for the care of his mother and announces that his mission is finished, offering his spirit to God. To make certain Jesus is dead, a soldier thrusts a spear in his side (John 19.25–37; Mark 15.33–41).

Jesus' death is the sacrifice needed to bring about the new covenant which God promised by the prophet Jeremiah (Jer. 31.31–34). The writer of the Letter to the Hebrews assures us that it is through Jesus' death that all who are penitent and have faith are forgiven (Heb. 9.1–28).

Deliberate on how the bread and wine of the Eucharist are Jesus' body and blood. Give thanks that his sacrifice gave us this new covenant of forgiveness and love.

Pray that you will accept God's forgiveness, a gift given freely for you – even if you think you're unworthy and know that you'll fall again.

Pray also that God will give you the strength and resources to resist temptation in the future.

13 The body is taken from the cross

Joseph of Arimathea, a Jewish councillor who believed the kingdom of God was about to come, and a secret admirer of Jesus, asks Pilate for Jesus' body. Surprised that Jesus is already dead, Pilate agrees, and Joseph removes the body from the cross and wraps it in a linen shroud that he provides (Mark 15.42–46a). John's Gospel says Joseph wraps the body in

Imagine how Joseph, Nicodemus and the women who were there felt when they took Jesus' tortured body from the cross. As well as their concern to bury him with dignity and due process before the Sabbath, their grief at his demise must have included anger at the way he had died unjustly in what, to them, must have seemed like a suicide mission.

strips or sheets of linen rather than a shroud like the Shroud of Turin, which many believe was Jesus' burial cloth. Accompanying Joseph is Nicodemus, who brings spices of myrrh and aloes to anoint the body (John 19.38–40).

14 Jesus is laid in the tomb

As Jesus' family were humble folk who came from Galilee, they would not have a family rock-hewn tomb in the limestone hillsides surrounding Jerusalem. So Joseph donates the use of his family tomb. It was customary in first-century Jerusalem for well-off people to lay out the body of a loved one on a slab in the tomb until the flesh rotted. After about a year, the family opened the tomb and, during a second burial service, placed the bones of the deceased in a limestone ossuary or bone box inside the tomb. Jesus' body is laid out in the vault, which is near the site of the crucifixion (John 19.40–42) – and most likely at the revered site within the Church of the Holy Sepulchre. A stone is rolled in front of the entrance. Mary Magdalene and Mary the mother of James the younger and Joses are witnesses to the burial (Mark 15.46–47).

Mull over the times you feel grief and anger at the way things don't work out the way you expect and ask God for patience and the ability to see his will in what is happening.

As Joseph pushes the stone across the sepulchre, all the hopes of what Jesus would accomplish seem doomed and buried. All his followers can do is show respect and reverence to the corpse of a good man and teacher.

There must be times when you've thought God is dead or has forsaken you. Think of when you felt despair and prayed that God would give you faith during these dark nights of the soul. Are you going through such a time now?

Give thanks for those who've died and whose faith has helped you in your Christian journey. Pray also for those who are dying, are in despair or have lost their faith, and for their ability to love with joy and enthusiasm.

Ask that God will resurrect you and all you pray for to new life in him.

● *Concluding prayer*

> O death, where is your sting? O grave, where is your victory?
> The sting of death is sin; and the strength of sin is the law.
> But thanks be to God, who gives us the victory through our Lord
>   Jesus Christ.
>
> (see 1 Cor. 15.55–57)

> Lord Jesus Christ, teach me to trust in you,
> to follow your example of faithfulness even to death.
> Take away my pride and foolish pretences.
> Thank you for forgiving my many faults through your sacrifice. May
>   I always be as forgiving to those who harm me and those I love.
> Show me how best I can witness to your love so that others may
>   come to know your saving grace.

Seven Last Words

While he was dying on the cross, the Gospels record how Jesus uttered seven short phrases. These last words are the springboard for meditating on Jesus' mission, especially during Lent and Easter, where they often form the basis of three-hour Good Friday church services. These services became popular with congregations during the nineteenth century. Composer Franz Joseph Haydn (1732–1809) produced sung orchestral and quartet versions of *The Seven Last Words of Christ* as a meditation, which are often performed on Good Friday.

As it uses only passages taken from the Gospels and has no set prayers or special structure, this meditation is popular with Protestants. Pastors can adapt the meditation on each of the phrases to the needs of their congregations while individuals can also use it for long or short periods for private meditations, pondering the meaning of Jesus' sacrifice. You can also meditate on each of the last sayings of Jesus by spending a day to a week on each at a time. Many people do this over the seven days of Holy Week, rather than just on Good Friday.

There are scores of books and online meditations on these famous last words that reflect the humanity of Jesus and divine salvation for us, taken from different perspectives. The words in the order they traditionally appear, as well as an explanation and suggested meditations are given in the table on pp. 107–12.

Father, forgive them, for they do not know what they are doing (Luke 23.34)

When Peter asks Jesus how often we should forgive, the answer Jesus gives is not seven times but 77 times (Matt. 18.21–23). In the Lord's Prayer, Jesus teaches us to pray for those who sin against us (Luke 11.4). He also tells us to love our enemies and to pray for those who persecute us (Matt. 5.43–45). His forgiving those who kill him is an example of his word in action.

Jesus' qualifying comment that 'they know not what they do' is a reference to how those responsible for his death have either misunderstood or rejected his mission.

Our own response to those who dislike or abuse us is either to defend, attack or to sulk. Maybe you try to justify yourself, spread stories that denigrate those who persecute you or ignore them as unworthy of your attention.

Jesus did none of these things. He recognized that we are all sinners loved by God and asked God to absolve those involved.

Think of several people with whom you don't get on, or who dislike you. Imagine them sitting beside you and think of how they, too, are created in God's image and how Jesus died for them as well as you. Ask God for a forgiving heart, pray for them and ask for guidance as to what action you can take.

I tell you the truth, today you will be with me in paradise (Luke 23.43)

Unlike those who were keen for Jesus to die, one of the two criminals crucified with him recognizes Jesus is innocent and asks to join him when his kingdom arrives. Jesus' reply, promising the criminal paradise, echoes how the wayward son is welcomed home in the parable of the prodigal son (Luke 15.11–32) and the parable of the labourers who start work at the eleventh hour and get the same pay as those who work all day (Matt. 20.1–16). Jesus

Most of us believe the greater the time and effort we put into something, the greater the reward. Having paid our dues, we expect our just deserts – if not in this life, then in the next. But Jesus is showing us that his kingdom is not about accruing points on a heavenly scorecard through how many times we've prayed or gone to church – or how many good deeds we've done. His kingdom is one of love that's open to all who will accept him.

is saying the kingdom of God is open to all who accept him – even those who come to him at the last minute.

This passage is popular at funeral services because it implies believers join Jesus in his heavenly kingdom in the afterlife as soon as they die.

However, Jesus could have meant that because his fellow sufferer had found redemption through him, he had discovered at the last minute paradise or true happiness similar to that which existed in the Garden of Eden before the Fall. Jesus' reference to how in his Father's house there 'are many rooms' and how he is going to prepare a place for us (John 14.1–3) could also be a reference to how there will always be room for the faithful and how he will return to us, rather than a promise of immediately entering a heavenly abode on death.

Think of when you've used your length of Christian 'service', your position in the Church, your good deeds or your high moral standards as giving you an edge over others. Note, also, how you might even feel superior about your own sense of humility.

Reflect also on the times you've been motivated by the hope of a heavenly reward rather than by your love of God.

To early Christians, pride was the greatest of the seven deadly sins. Ask for God's forgiveness and help for you to accept that we are all sinners in need of redemption through his amazing grace.

When Jesus saw his mother there, and the disciple whom he loved standing nearby, he said to his mother, 'Dear woman, here is your son,' and to the disciple, 'Here is your mother.' From that time on, this disciple took her into his home (John 19.26–27)

In keeping with the fifth commandment to honour your father and mother (Exod. 20.12; Deut. 5.16), Jesus arranges for the care of his mother, now in her late forties or early fifties.

Many scholars believe the Apostle John is the disciple whom Jesus loved. Tradition suggests the Virgin Mary went to Ephesus in modern Turkey and John cared for her there. Other traditions say she remained in Jerusalem.

The Gospel accounts vary as to the women near the foot of the cross. John's Gospel mentions three Marys: Jesus' mother; her sister, Mary the wife of Clopas; and Mary Magdalene. There's no mention of Jesus' mother in Mark and the other Gospels. But they do mention women who followed him from Galilee: Mary Magdalene, Mary the mother of James the younger and of Joses, and the mother of Zebedee's sons, and Salome.

Unlike most of the disciples who seem to have abandoned Jesus out of fear that they, too, will suffer the same fate, the women who've followed him from Galilee remain supportive. Reflect on their example and ask God for this virtue of dedicated love and service to him.

Even though he's in the throes of death, Jesus is still the dutiful son who hands the care of his mother over to the disciple with whom he has a special relationship. Remember the times when you've been under pressure, stress or suffered an illness and how you can become so focused on your own needs that you forget your duty to God and the needs of others. Ask for forgiveness, then think of one or two positive steps you might take in the future and ask for God's guidance and help.

If they are still alive, ponder on how you treat your own parents. Do they have any needs that you've been ignoring? How often do you visit them or let them know how much you love them? Think also about how you treat other members of your family and what steps you can take to improve the relationship. If necessary, ask for forgiveness and pray for them and for God's direction.

And at the ninth hour Jesus cried out in a loud voice, 'Eloi, Eloi, lama sabachthani?' – which means, 'My God, my God, why have you forsaken me?' (Mark 15.34)

Jesus' cry is in his native Aramaic, the language the Jews learned in exile in Babylon from 597 to 537 BC and continued to use when they returned to the Holy Land. Jesus repeats the opening words of Psalm 22, which starts with complaints that God does not heed the call of his servant – and then switches to praise for God, including how all the nations shall turn to God and worship him.

At some stage, most of us feel forsaken by God and that we're facing a hostile world. Maybe those we love and trust have let us down.

But has God forsaken you? Or have you forsaken God? Or are you demanding a sign from God? Deliberate on when you yourself forsake God. Maybe you've been ashamed of being a Christian, have been too busy or swapped God for other pursuits and people. Ask for forgiveness and make several practical resolutions – that you know you can achieve – that will bring you closer to God, and ask for his help. Then praise God and give thanks for all he does.

Jesus said, 'I am thirsty' (John 19.28)

Jesus rarely mentions his own physical needs and his thirst is a clear sign of his humanity. A sponge soaked in sour wine or vinegar is pressed to his lips on the end of a branch of the bitter-tasting herb hyssop. This experience is similar to that of the psalmist, who describes receiving vinegar to drink as he suffers (Ps. 69.21).

We are usually more attuned to our own desires and wishes than the needs of others. How often do you listen and respond to the pleas of those who are hungry, thirsty, strangers, ill-clothed or imprisoned and abused (Matt. 25.31–46)? Add to these needy people those who are dissatisfied with their materialist lifestyle and suffer from spiritual thirst.

The irony of Jesus' acknowledging his thirst is that he told the Samaritan woman at the well that those who receive the waters he will give them will never thirst (John 4.1–15). He also told his disciples that whoever believes in him would never thirst.

Jesus reprimanded Peter for defending him with a sword, reasoning with Peter that he must drink the cup his Father has given him (John 18.10–11). Perhaps the thirst Jesus is referring to is quenched by the cup his Father has given him, which requires the ultimate sacrifice of death.

Jesus said, 'It is finished' (John 19.30)

Before he finally expires, Jesus announces that his mission is finished or complete.
His death will be the fulfilment of the task God sent him to do.

It's easy for those of us who are more fortunate to offer excuses or ignore the plight of others. Imagine Jesus thirsty on the cross, then look into your heart and reflect on the ways you might be avoiding responding to those in need.

Ask for God's forgiveness and then settle on some positive ways that you will respond to these needs. Maybe it will mean giving money or doing volunteer work for a particular charity, doing further research into a human rights issue or making a substantial investment of yourself or your resources. It may also mean befriending someone thirsty for God and including them in your prayers, or considering what missionary work you can do. Ask for God's guidance and direction in keeping your resolve.

How often do we pull back from completing the mission that God sets us? Jesus told the parable of the sower (Matt. 13.1–9) and gave other examples to illustrate how we can easily fall by the wayside.

Jesus called out with a loud voice, 'Father, into your hands I commit my spirit.' When he had said this, he breathed his last (Luke 23.46)

Having completed his mission, Jesus surrenders himself to his inevitable death by repeating a phrase from a psalm offering the one who prays to God (Ps. 31.5).

As Jesus is repeating a Hebrew psalm, he is not referring to a spiritual soul that will continue to exist apart from his body after he dies, but to how he is entrusting or giving back all his life and energy to his Father. The word 'spirit' is associated with breath or wind and in the Hebrew Bible God breathes life into us and takes it away (e.g. Gen. 2.7).

Ask yourself, 'If I were facing death in a few minutes, could I put my hand on my heart and say, "I've stayed on course and done my best, with God's help, to fulfil what he wanted me to do"?' Most of us couldn't.

In what ways do you go off course? Is there something you can learn from this? How might you use these experiences to God's advantage? Does God want you to go in a new direction?

Be still for a while and listen to what God might want you to do next. Don't expect an immediate answer, but offer all your ideas to God and ask for his guidance.

Jesus offers his life back to his Father, which is a parable for how we need to offer God's gift of our lives back to him for his use out of love.

Offer all that you are to God – including your experiences, abilities, energy and time – for his kingdom and ask for his direction.

St Paul tells us that God has offered Jesus as a gift to free us from the mistakes we make that distance us from God so that we can become reconciled to him (Rom. 6.22–23). Accept that Jesus has given his life for you. Rejoice, give thanks and praise to God for this wonderful gift of love.

Before diving headlong into a meditation on these last words, don't forget to place yourself in the presence of the Lord (see 'Making contact', pp. 27–30, 'Imagining his presence', pp. 25–7 and 'Salesian devotion', pp. 114–16).

Here are some further suggestions that you may also find helpful.

Ask God to open your heart and mind to his Word. Then, seek his guidance in your meditation so that you gain new insights into his love for you and for all others. Ask that he inspire you to come up with positive ways in which you can respond to that love.

To help focus on Jesus' last hours and their significance, use as a prayer Isaac Watts' (1674–1748) well-known hymn, 'When I survey the wondrous cross'.

> When I survey the wondrous cross,
> On which the Prince of glory died,
> My richest gain I count but loss,
> And pour contempt on all my pride.
>
> Forbid it, Lord, that I should boast
> Save in the death of Christ my God;
> All the vain things that charm me most,
> I sacrifice them to His blood.
>
> See from His head, His hands, His feet,
> Sorrow and love flow mingled down;
> Did e'er such love and sorrow meet,
> Or thorns compose so rich a crown?
>
> His dying crimson, like a robe,
> Spreads o'er His body on the Tree;
> Then am I dead to all the globe,
> And all the globe is dead to me.
>
> Were the whole realm of nature mine,
> That were a present far too small;
> Love so amazing, so divine,
> Demands my soul, my life, my all.

When you finish your meditations, ask that God will give you the motivation and focus to carry out any resolutions you've made. Aim to carry them out as soon as possible, preferably within a day or two.

End with the Lord's Prayer and then the *Gloria Patri*:

Glory be to the Father and to the Son and to the Holy Spirit.
As it was in the beginning, is now and ever shall be,
world without end. Amen.

Salesian devotion

'It may be that you don't know how to pray mentally . . . for unfortunately this is something that few people in our time know how to do,' wrote the French bishop, St Francis de Sales (1567–1622), in his highly popular spiritual classic *Introduction to the Devout Life*, first published in 1609, which is constantly being republished. He decided to remedy this situation by offering one of the first practical prayer guides for the laity. It contains plenty of good advice and meditations, including a simply structured meditation technique, which he divided into preparation, consideration of the chosen subject, affections and resolutions, and conclusion and spiritual bouquet.

Preparation

Francis regarded preparation as important and gave several steps to begin.

Choose a suitable topic, such as a mystery of the faith – the Trinity, the Eucharist, God's love, the incarnation of God in Jesus – or a Gospel theme. A mystery of the faith, by its very nature, is going to appear abstract and difficult to understand. But don't let this put you off. Each time you meditate on a particular mystery, you're likely to gain further insights.

Now, begin your meditation by placing yourself in the presence of God, using one of these four ways:

- Recognize that God is everywhere and is present in all things.
- Remember that God is especially present 'in your heart and in the very centre of your spirit'.
- Imagine Jesus looking down from heaven while you are at prayer.
- Imagine that Jesus is actually present within you, as you would imagine a friend present.

Francis advises not to mix these preparations and use them all at once, 'but only one at a time and that briefly and simply'.

In the second part of the preparation, ask for God's assistance 'in order to serve and adore him properly in this meditation'. St Francis also suggests that you could ask for guidance from your guardian angel or a saint. Your saint might be the Virgin Mary if you're meditating on the nativity, or St John or Mary Magdalene if you selected the crucifixion.

The final part of the preparation is to visualize the mystery or Gospel scene as if it were taking place before your eyes (see 'The time machine', pp. 81–4). This is not essential to the meditation and may be difficult for abstract themes like God's greatness, the purpose of creation or God's eternal existence.

Considerations

After your preparation, the next stage is to select one or two points from the topic of your meditation and reflect on their meaning. If you choose the stoning of St Stephen (Acts 7.54–60), for instance, you could highlight the way this martyr was prepared to go to his death while forgiving his persecutors. If you find enough substance in just one point, remain with it, but don't feel obliged to squeeze your subject dry. Francis suggests we imitate the bee.

> And if your mind finds sufficient matter, light and fruit wherein to rest in any one consideration, dwell upon it, even as the bee, which hovers over one flower so long as it affords honey. But if you do not find wherewith to feed your mind, after a certain reasonable effort, then go on to another consideration, – only be quiet and simple, and do not be eager or hurried.

Affections and resolutions

The meditation is likely to produce feelings of love for God and a desire to do his will. But you'll need to turn these feelings into specific resolutions – things you plan to do with God's help. In the example of St Stephen's martyrdom, you could try to imitate him by seeking the courage to be steadfast in the faith and to be forgiving and to reconcile yourself with those who've made disparaging remarks about your beliefs or even discriminated against you because of your faith. You may also consider those many Christians persecuted today for their faith and in what ways you can support them.

Conclusion and spiritual bouquet

In concluding your meditation, thank God for what you have learned and for the resolutions he has given you. Then offer to him your desire to carry out the resolutions and ask him to bless them.

Francis de Sales suggests at this point praying for the Church, clergy, relatives, friends and others who need our intercessions.

Next, you could pray the Lord's Prayer or the Hail Mary.

Finally, choose one or two points you've been meditating on to savour throughout the day. Francis calls this 'a little bouquet of devotion', or 'spiritual bouquet'.

> When walking in a beautiful garden most people are wont to gather a few flowers as they go, which they keep, and enjoy their scent during the day. So, when the mind explores some mystery in meditation, it is well to pick out one or more points that have specially arrested the attention, and are most likely to be helpful to you through the day, and this should be done at once before quitting the subject of your meditation.

After you've finished your meditation, Francis suggests keeping still for a while before gradually adjusting your mind to your other activities.

Francis emphasizes how important it is to carry out your spiritual resolutions and intentions the same day of your meditation. He tells us this is the fruit of our endeavour and that we should look for different ways, both small and great, of putting this into practice. He suggests that if you've resolved to win over someone who's offended you, then you'll try to meet and be friendly to that person and, if that's not possible, to pray for them.

Putting off your resolutions until another date is definitely out as far as Francis is concerned. You're less likely to act on them and you might feel good about yourself for having merely meditated, even though you've avoided doing what the Holy Spirit has called on you to do.

Sulpician approach

'To have Jesus before the eyes, in the heart and in the hands: that is the whole Christian life.' This comment of Fr Louis Tronson (1622–1700) summarizes the essence of the Sulpician method of meditation. It's part of the French school of spirituality that's had a major influence on the Catholic Church through its emphasis on personal devotions, a personal experience of Jesus and the need to seek holiness. This form of spirituality originated with Cardinal Pierre de Bérulle (1575–1629) and Fr Jean-Jacques Olier (1608–57), who founded the Society of St Sulpice in Paris in 1641 to manage seminaries and train priests.

The heart of the Sulpician approach is adoring Christ and his virtues, making these virtues your own and trying to live by them: adoration, communion and cooperation. Fr Tronson, the third superior general of the seminary at St Sulpice, added some extra material: preparation, considerations and self-examination, as well as a conclusion. It's his version that's outlined here, with slight modifications as the original text was intended for seminarians.

Preparation

Ideally, you should begin your preparation the night before. Select one of Jesus' virtues: humility, compassion, obedience, love, mercy, persistence, integrity, self-discipline. To give you inspiration, you could refer to relevant passages in the New Testament, especially the Gospels. Keep the topic in mind as you go to sleep, and expect to do your meditation soon after rising.

When you're ready to meditate, place yourself in the Lord's presence (see 'Salesian devotion', p. 114), recognizing before him your own unworthiness and dependence. Then call upon the Holy Spirit to guide you. You could also pray the *Veni Creator Spiritus*, originally written in the ninth century and the most famous of all hymns. It's in many prayer books and hymnals and is also available on the Internet. Here is one version:

> Come, Creator, Spirit,
> visit the souls of your own;
> fill with heavenly grace
> the breasts that you have created.
>
> You who are called Paraclete,
> gift of the most high God,
> living water, flame, charity,
> and spiritual anointing;
>
> You who are sevenfold in your gift,
> finger of God's right hand,
> you who were rightly promised by the Father,
> enrich our throats with speech.
>
> Inflame the light of our senses,
> pour love into our hearts,

the weakness of our bodies
strengthen with lasting power.

Drive the enemy far back,
and at once grant us peace;
with you going ahead of us,
may we avoid all harm.

Through you may we know the Father
and recognize the Son;
and may we always believe in you,
Spirit of both.

Body of the prayer/meditation

Adoration: Jesus before your eyes

Think about the subject you have chosen in a general way so it becomes a backdrop to enable you to dwell on the incarnate Lord – the person of Jesus. If you choose Jesus' humility, don't get sidetracked by the details of what happened during the nativity at the stable in Bethlehem or analysing the minutiae of what took place at the Last Supper when Jesus washed his disciples' feet (John 13.1–17). In other words, don't think about the kind of basin used, where he got his water from or the symbolic significance of Peter's comments. Instead, offer Jesus your heartfelt feelings of adoration, admiration, praise, love, joy and gratitude.

Communion: Jesus in the heart

After you've cherished this virtue in Jesus, consider ways in which you lack this good quality and then open your heart to let the virtue become part of you. Fr Tronson compares this process with receiving the bread and wine of the Eucharist. 'As we commune with the body of our Lord when we open the mouth and receive him', he says, 'so we commune with his virtues and his spirit when opening the mouth of our soul; we receive him in the heart.'

Cooperation: Jesus in your hands

Having received the virtue in your heart, make a specific resolution to carry this out in your life. You are cooperating with God in putting this virtue into practice. Set yourself realistic goals and go about fulfilling them as soon as you can.

Conclusion

Thank God for all the good things you've received during your meditation and ask forgiveness for any lack of attention or half-heartedness. Ask him to bless your resolutions. Finally, select a thought to carry with you during the rest of your day as a spiritual bouquet.

Spiritual Exercises

The commander wanted to surrender to the French, but Inigo de Loyola (1491–1556), an officer with a reputation for womanizing and brawling, convinced him to fight on for the honour of Spain. When the much larger French force conquered the citadel at Pamplona, 30-year-old Inigo, or Ignatius, received serious wounds in one leg and had the other fractured by a cannon ball. The leg was set badly and a bone protruded, so, not wishing to look deformed at court, Ignatius insisted it be broken and set again – without the benefit of anaesthetic. While recuperating at home, Ignatius admits in his *Autobiography* (written in the third person) to asking for romance novels to entertain himself and how he daydreamed of impressing a lady of the highest nobility with his exploits and charm. He says the only literature available was *The Life of Christ* by Rudolph the Carthusian and another book called the *Flowers of the Saints*, which had a profound influence on him. As the days passed, he alternated his thinking between worldly and spiritual matters.

> When he thought of worldly things it gave him great pleasure, but afterward he found himself dry and sad. But when he thought of journeying to Jerusalem, and of living only on herbs, and practising austerities, he found pleasure not only while thinking of them, but also when he had ceased. (*Autobiography*)

This revelation was the beginning of Ignatius' spiritual journey. He experienced visions and struggled with temptation as he tried to discern between godly, selfish and evil spirits to determine the true will of God.

Ignatius gave up his military and romantic aspirations and put all his energy into trying to be like the saints he had read about, especially St Francis of Assisi. He began living a simple ascetic life dedicated to prayer, penance and teaching the faith. Like St Francis, he made a pilgrimage to the Holy Land, trusting God to provide. Upon returning to Spain, his teachings and practices brought him to the attention of the Spanish Inquisition. He suffered a short period of imprisonment and studied for seven years before ordination.

In 1534, he and six others founded the Society of Jesus, or the Jesuits, at St Mary's Church, Montmartre, in Paris. The Jesuits took a major role in the Counter-Reformation through their high level of education and missionary work in Europe and helped spread the gospel to Asia and South America. Today, Jesuits are active in 112 countries.

St Ignatius' greatest impact on spirituality is that he recognized that there's more to prayer than reciting verses. From his own spiritual journey, he knew how it involves the conversion of the heart and feelings as well as the intellect, so that they and personal experiences become part of God in our lives – and his Spiritual Exercises reflect this. Written between 1522 and 1524 while studying for ordination at the University of Paris, the Spiritual Exercises are a collection of prayers, imaginative meditations, examination of conscience, and reflective exercises that take place with the help of a spiritual director during a secluded thirty-day, four-week retreat.

Originally intended as part of the initial training for Jesuits, it is sometimes condensed to a weekend or eight-day retreat, or you might like to take a week to do each daily exercise – a thirty-week exercise that you do in the privacy of your home.

Here's an overview with the essence of the four weeks, or phases, that Ignatius outlines in the Spiritual Exercises. If you can't do the full Ignatius-style retreat, use it as a basis for a longer and progressive meditation that will help to recognize your weaknesses and strengths and convert you to becoming more Christ-like.

The aim of each of the four phases is to:

1 change sinful patterns of behaviour;
2 model your behaviour on that of Jesus;
3 reinforce what conforms with the ways of Jesus;
4 infuse your Christ-like intentions with love and devotion.

Phase 1: Principle and foundation

(a) 'Man is created to praise, reverence, and serve God our Lord, and by this means to save his soul. And the other things on the face of the earth are created for man and that they may help him in prosecuting the end for which he is created' (*Spiritual Exercises*

23). Focus on how God has revealed himself in creation. Then consider how he reveals himself in the events of history and how much he reaches out to us in love, especially through his Son, Jesus.

(b) Recognize what is sinful and alienates us from God's love. It may help to read the Ten Commandments and Jesus' summary of the Law in the two commandments of love of God and neighbour.

(c) Now you need to be honest to God about your own shortcomings, mistakes and other negative lifestyle patterns. Remember to include your thoughts as well as actions. 'Ask grace to know our sins and cast them out' (*Spiritual Exercises* 43). Examine your own conscience, perhaps with the help of a spiritual director, so that you go beyond excuses, rationalizations and other justifications for your unloving attitudes and behaviour. It may help to go through each of the seven deadly sins: lust, gluttony, greed, sloth, anger, envy, pride.

(d) Accept that despite your faults, like any loving parent, God still loves you and wants you to respond with love. Your heartfelt desire to respond to God's generous love leads to the second phase of wanting to serve him.

Phase 2: The call of the kingdom

(a) Think of what a sovereign expects from his or her subjects.

(b) Read the Bible and learn of Jesus' call to work for the kingdom of God.

(c) Ask yourself how God wants you to respond to this call and how you can accompany Jesus in this task.

(d) Imagine scenes from Jesus' life that will stir an affection and desire to be like Jesus.

> In order to imitate and be more actually like Christ our Lord, I want and choose poverty with Christ poor rather than riches, opprobrium with Christ replete with it rather than honours; and to desire to be rated as worthless and a fool for Christ, Who first was held as such, rather than wise or prudent in this world.
>
> (*Spiritual Exercises* 167)

(e) Pay particular attention to the values or virtues that Jesus shows, such as faithfulness, avoiding succumbing to temptation, going the extra mile, compassion, mercy, willingness to evangelize and embrace all, teaching, healing, and so on.

(f) Note any opposition you might feel about imitating Jesus, remembering that the teachings and choices Jesus made are God's will for you, too.

(g) Through meditating on the life and values of Jesus, let go of what you hold dear and let him convert you so that his values become your values.

Phase 3: Reflecting on the passion

(a) After answering the call to befriend and follow Jesus, like his disciples did, look again at what the Bible has to say about his passion – from the time of preparation for his last meal with his disciples until his crucifixion. This will probably make you feel sad to know that someone you love seems powerless to save himself from an unjust and untimely death.

(b) Ask God that you, too, may have the kind of compassion that Jesus had, especially when he was on the cross.

(c) As Jesus suffered for all humankind, widen your horizons to all who suffer.

(d) Empathize with Jesus and his suffering. 'Consider how He suffers all this for my sins, etc.; and what I ought to do and suffer for Him' (*Spiritual Exercises* 197).

(e) Surrender yourself to God as Jesus did, whatever the cost, giving yourself out of love.

Phase 4: The peace, love and joy of Jesus

(a) Imagine and reflect on scenes associated with Jesus taken down from the cross, his burial, resurrection and ascension.

(b) Be open to experience the joy of the resurrection and to how God has revealed his love through Jesus. 'Consider how the Divinity, which seemed to hide Itself in the Passion, now appears and shows Itself so marvellously in the most holy Resurrection by Its true and most holy effects' (*Spiritual Exercises* 223).

(c) Recognize how God is with you in all your experiences, whether they are good or bad, joyful or sorrowful.

(d) Be grateful for what God has done for you and seek to discover his presence in all creation. This will take you beyond the privacy of your own life to relate with others and proclaim his kingdom to others.

Here's how you undertake each day's meditation.

Topic for meditation

Choose a topic from events in the Bible – especially from the life of Jesus – and identify what you intend to gain from this meditation.

Preparation

Every day, before you begin each meditation, place yourself in the presence of God and open yourself to his revealing himself to you.

Composition of place

This is where you use art works, your imagination and all your senses – sight, hearing, touch, taste, feeling – concentrating on one sense at a time, to imagine yourself as one of the people participating in the scene so it reveals spiritual insights to you and how you should respond to God (see 'The time machine', pp. 82–4).

For example, in Phase 3 Ignatius asks you to imagine the events surrounding the Last Supper. Feel grief at Jesus' suffering for your sins. Watch, listen, touch, taste and learn from how the disciples react. Note how Jesus hid his divinity rather than destroy his enemies and then ask yourself 'what I ought to do and suffer for Him' (*Spiritual Exercises* 197).

Prayer

Your prayer and meditations are your reflections on what you've imagined. Trust in God to guide and give you the desires that he seeks for you and be open to discern what he wants. Avoid forcing these revelations or always expecting something profound from the biblical scene you imagine.

Application of the senses: Revisit the experiences that had the most impact on you and apply your senses so that you relish what's happening to you in more detail – so that you can come closer to God and his desires for you.

Colloquy

At the end of each exercise, pray to God as if you're having a discussion with a loving friend. Mention what has happened during your meditations and ask for guidance. You may also want to discuss with your spiritual director what happened. End your colloquy with the Lord's Prayer.

Action

The insights and desire to be more Christ-like that you gained through the exercises will lead you to re-engage with your regular life with gratitude for his sacrifice and love. It will make you aware of the importance of life, your own mortality and the need to spread God's kingdom of love with humility and gratitude for the gift of life God has given you as you imitate Christ with enthusiasm.

6
ASIAN PRAYER METHODS

Yoga

Many Christians are suspicious of the methods of other religions. They feel that if they borrow the method, they must also accept the doctrine. That simply isn't true. Christianity throughout its history has absorbed and adapted customs and ideas of other religions and philosophies and has taken the best from them to use to the glory of God. The ancient Hindu practice of yoga is a typical example of an Asian prayer method that some Christians have modified and use as a Christian meditation technique.

In Sanskrit yoga means 'yoke', the uniting of body, mind and soul to the Divine Spirit. It is a means of controlling the mind and senses so that we can be in harmony with God and ourselves. The ancient Hindu scriptures, the *Upanishads*, describe it this way:

> When all senses are stilled, when the mind is at rest, when the intellect wavers not – then, say the wise, is reached the highest state. This calm of the senses and the mind has been defined as yoga. He who attains it is freed from delusion.   (*Kathopanishad*)

Although yoga is mentioned in these pre-fifth-century BC scriptures, it was not until the second century BC that Patanjali developed it into a systematic method. During the Victorian era, the Theosophical Society in the United Kingdom became interested in Hinduism, including yoga. But it wasn't until Indian immigrants came to England from the late 1940s that yoga gained popularity in the West.

In the 1880s, Swami Vivekenanda (1863–1902) – who founded the Vedanta Society, a Hindu movement that attracted many literary figures in the 1950s, such as Aldous Huxley (1894–1963) – introduced yoga to the United States. The religious elements, however, have generally taken a back seat in the Western world, where yoga is promoted as a means to health and serenity rather than union with God. Nevertheless, some Christians have adopted yoga routines when they pray, replacing the Hindu concept of the Universal Spirit with the Holy Trinity.

There are various forms of yoga:

- hatha yoga, the basic form emphasizing breathing and posture exercises;
- karma yoga, the way of action;

- jnana yoga, the way of knowledge;
- bhakti yoga, the way of devotion and faith;
- japa yoga, which emphasizes mantra chanting;
- laya or kundalini yoga, which concentrates on hidden power centres within the body;
- raja yoga, literally 'the king of yoga', which combines many elements from the other schools in an eight-point programme.

The eight points or limbs of kundalini yoga include observing moral commandments, self-discipline and purification, postures, controlled breathing, detachment, concentration on a fixed point, meditation and Samadhi or super-conscious union with the subject of contemplation. Fr Herbert Slade of the Anglican Society of St John the Evangelist, or the Cowley Fathers as they are better known, describes in *Exploration into Contemplative Prayer* how many in his religious order had customized these eight limbs for the Christian contemplative life. The programme is too involved to summarize here but if you're interested in embracing a yogic style of prayer, it's worth examining.

The form of yoga that's become popular in the West is the simplest and most basic, hatha yoga, which emphasizes the breathing exercises or pranayamas and 84 stylized postures or asanas. Here's a basic hatha yoga breathing exercise. You might like to try it to help you relax, be more alert and able to concentrate during prayer.

Lie on your back on the floor and exhale, pulling in your abdomen as tightly as you can to expel the air through your mouth and nose. When you feel there's no more air left, imagine you have a birthday cake with the candles ablaze and try to blow them all out. Then, as though there were one more candle, blow again without taking another breath. Your lungs should now be empty. Then close your mouth and begin breathing through your nose, trying to fill your lungs completely. Now breathe out through your nostrils and repeat the process until you feel a little light-headed. (This is because of the oversupply of oxygen to the brain.) Relax for a while, then try the procedure several more times.

Next, you might try some of the postures. It is preferable to receive training from a competent teacher or guru, one who can take you from darkness (*gu*) towards enlightenment (*ru* = light). You might also learn the basics from one of the many self-instruction manuals (see 'Further reading'). Don't feel compelled to master all the postures. For Christians, the most valuable will be the lotus position or one of its variations. Because the spine is in perfect alignment and the circulation remains unimpeded, this sitting position provides the best way of keeping the body still for prolonged periods of prayer. For this reason, it is ideal for extended meditation and contemplation. As the lotus is a unique position, it can serve to put you in a prayerful mood, in the same way that visiting a chapel might.

The half-lotus is the best way to begin.

1 Sit on the floor with your legs outstretched. You might prefer to sit on a small cushion or even a telephone book to help you get into position and avoid resting on your heels.
2 Grasp your left foot in your hands and place your left heel against the perineum (the area between the genitals and the anus), with the sole against the inside of your right thigh.
3 Now bend the right leg and cross it over the left ankle, keeping the right heel against the abdomen.
4 Position the sole of your right foot in the cleft between the thigh and calf of your left leg.
5 Rest your hands on your knees.

At first, you'll be lucky if you can get your legs in place and keep your knees on the floor. As your muscles will need to loosen and stretch, you'll need to ease yourself into the half-lotus position over a period of weeks. Your knees will almost certainly hurt on your early attempts, but don't force yourself to do anything that's too painful. Limbering up first with leg-stretching exercises might prove helpful.

Once you've mastered the half-lotus, you could consider graduating to the full lotus.

1 Sit on the floor with legs outstretched, as in the half-lotus.
2 Grasp the right foot and place it at the base of the thigh so that your right heel is near your navel.
3 Grasp your left foot and bring it over the right leg to the base of your right thigh, the heel being near the navel.
4 Check that the soles of both feet face upward.
5 To extricate yourself from this posture, reverse the procedure.

It is advisable to alternate the legs from time to time.

If you wish to go beyond the physical aspects of hatha yoga, you might like to try some of the concentration, meditation and contemplative techniques of raja yoga. A favourite discipline for strengthening the ability to concentrate is the candle exercise.

Place a lighted candle about a metre in front of you. Gaze directly at the flame for about two minutes. Then close your eyes and cover them with the palms of your hands. For the next two minutes, retain the mental image of the flame. Try not to let the image disappear, but if this happens, without looking at the candle again, try to recall it in your imagination. Repeat this each time your mind begins to wander. With practice, you'll be able to minimize distractions altogether – a skill that can be readily transferred to your prayer life – by seeing the flame as the 'light of the world' (John 8.12; 9.5). Or, noting how Jesus said, 'You are the light of the world' (Matt. 5.14), see the candle as the Holy Spirit illuminating you and, through you, others.

Yoga meditations are often divided into those with 'seed' – in which we are actively focusing on a thought, image or object – or 'seedless' – in which the mind is emptied of all ideas and images and is filled with a simple awareness of God. One meditation with seed is the multi-petal lotus flower. Here is a Christian form of this exercise.

When you are completely relaxed, select a word which has a Christian connotation: a cross, bread, wine, water, blood, tomb, mercy. Make this word the centre of your lotus and let an association come freely to mind. If you choose wine for the lotus centre, you might make the connection with grapes. This association would be the first petal of the lotus. Make your association a fleeting one of less than five seconds as this is not an in-depth meditation. Now, return to the centre and make a new association, your second petal. Avoid linking associations with petal words. This time wine might suggest the blood of Christ. Next time it could be corkscrew, then bottle, pizza and the wedding feast at Cana (John 2.1–11). You can't always foresee which direction these associations will take. Don't forget to go back to the centre before adding another petal word or phrase. Continue this exercise for about a quarter of an hour. When you're finished, you'll probably be surprised at the connections you've made, and this will often give you insights into yourself and your faith.

A seedless meditation is a form of mystical contemplation. In Hindu practice, this involves rising above all conscious thoughts and images to reach a state of harmony with creation and ourselves. 'There remains no sense of "I" or "mine," as the working of the body, the mind and the intellect have stopped as if one is in a deep sleep,' explains B. K. S. Iyengar (1918–), probably the foremost yoga teacher in the world. He adds,

> There is only the experience of consciousness, truth and unutterable joy. There is peace that passeth all understanding . . . Yoga has departed from the material world and has merged with the eternal. There is then no duality between the knower and the known, for they are merged like camphor and the flame.   (*Light of Yoga*, p. 54)

If you use yoga methods for mystical contemplation, aim to actively surrender to God's love and his will rather than passively accepting your place in creation.

Zen

'What is the sound of one hand clapping?' This well-known riddle has become something of a cliché for Zen meditation. Yet, it is the kind of puzzle a Zen master might give a pupil to lead him or her toward enlightenment or satori, the aim of Zen. Some Christians also use the meditation methods of Zen to help with their prayer life and gain insights into the gospel.

Zen is a sect of Mahayana Buddhism, the Northern School, which according to legend was brought to China in the sixth century by the Indian philosopher Bodhidharma, from where it spread to Japan in the twelfth century. It was introduced into the United States at the World Parliament of Religions at the Chicago Exposition in 1893. But it didn't gain popularity in Western countries until the 1950s when it featured in several books, including the 1953 account of martial arts training in Eugen Herrigel's *Zen in the Art of Archery* and Jack Kerouac's *The Dharma Bums*, published in 1959. Trappist monk and spiritual writer Thomas Merton (1915–68) drew many parallels between Zen and Christian spirituality.

With Zen, enlightenment comes through an intuitive experience rather than through rational thought. One of the best-known authorities on Zen, Daisetz Suzuki (1870–1966), who translated Japanese Zen writings into English and helped spread Zen to the West, says that 'with satori our entire surroundings are viewed from quite an unexpected angle of perception. Whatever this is, the world for those who have gained a satori is no more the old world it used to be' (*Zen Buddhism*, p. 84). In a minor way, we can experience satori when, after wrestling with a problem for many days, the solution comes all at once – the light suddenly dawns and we have a 'eureka' experience.

This new insight is unlikely to be an emotional or cataclysmic affair like St Paul's conversion on the road to Damascus (Acts 9.1–8). A Zen student can experience many satoris, gaining a new revelation each time. The Zen master, or roshi, guides the student toward enlightenment through a series of questions, making certain their satoris are genuine and not imitations, and that students don't become obsessed with a particular experience. Because Buddhists don't believe in a deity, the satori doesn't provide an insight into the divine.

There are two paths to satori: zazen, or the sitting discipline of meditation, and the koans, the paradoxical riddles. Often these activities happen together. Zazen helps to still the restless mind, which is like a chattering monkey, so that we can go beyond our self-image to come to terms with our true nature.

Here's a basic zazen exercise on the breath. Sit in a comfortable position – the lotus, half-lotus or on a straight-backed chair – and make sure your head, back and neck are in a straight line. Spend a few minutes becoming aware of your bodily sensations.

With your mouth closed, focus all your attention on your breathing so that you are aware of the air moving in and out of your nostrils. Let it flow naturally and avoid letting your consciousness of your breathing change the way you breathe.

After a few moments, begin to count each breath silently like this: one and two and three and four and so on. Count 'one' on the inhalation and 'and' on the exhalation, then 'two' on the next inhalation and 'and' on the exhalation and so on, up to ten. The counting is merely an aid to focusing on the breath. So, if you lose your place, just return to 'one' again. Continue this exercise for 15 to 20 minutes.

In the book of Genesis, we learn that God blew life into human beings. It is the presence of his breath, or the Spirit of God, which keeps us alive. When God takes breath away, death follows. Father Anthony de Mello (1931–87) a controversial Jesuit from India, some of whose views were considered at variance with and harmful to the Catholic faith, offered this interesting variation: 'While you breathe out, imagine you are breathing out all your impurities . . . your fears . . . your negative feelings' (*Sadhana: A Way to God*, p. 32).

The other main route to satori is through the koans. A roshi normally selects a suitable koan, from about 1,700, for an individual student. These seemingly nonsensical riddles – Does the dog have Buddha nature? What was your original face before your parents conceived you? If all things can be reduced to one, to what can one be reduced? – are merely a means to opening the door to satori. Zen masters compare the koan to a brick 'with which to knock at a door; when the door is opened, the brick may be thrown away' (*The Spirit of Zen*, p. 71). Usually the student will begin to approach the koan in an intellectual way, looking for symbolic meanings and associations to try to arrive at a logical solution. A breakthrough can come only when the thinking process is put aside.

Christians who are familiar with Zen koans have found their experiences have given them insights into the baffling paradoxes of the Bible. Father J. K. Kadowaki treats these sayings of Jesus in a similar way to koans:

> It is easier for a camel to go through the eye of a needle than for a rich man to enter the kingdom of God. (Mark 10.25)

> I tell you the truth, unless a grain of wheat falls to the ground and dies, it remains only a single seed. But if it dies, it produces many seeds. (John 12.24)

William Johnston, author of *Christian Zen*, also considers the following as Christian koans:

> Let the dead bury their own dead. (Matt. 8.22)

> For whoever wants to save his life will lose it, but whoever loses his life for me and for the gospel will save it. (Mark 8.35)

> This is my body. (Mark 14.22; 1 Cor. 11.24)

Although Zen koans are understood in an intuitive way, most of the Christian paradoxes that are thought to resemble koans are in fact only apparent contradictions and can usually be understood rationally. Nevertheless, the methods of Zen can help attain inner stillness and to go beyond reason to give different perspectives to what the gospel message can mean to us personally.

7

PRAYING IN TONGUES

Praying in tongues

'I was so filled with the Holy Spirit the words just flowed.' This was how one man described his experience of praying in tongues. The words he spoke sounded like an exotic language, which few, if any, would understand: *'By yung bah stay les krostanday shong doh foh. Bing dy kray.'*

Speaking in tongues or glossolalia – a term first coined in 1879 by Frederic W. Farrar (1831–1903) – is alluded to in the Hebrew Bible, or Old Testament, in the book of the prophet Isaiah (Isa. 28.11). St Peter says the speaking in tongues at Pentecost is what the prophet Joel was referring to (Acts 2.14–40; Joel 2.28–32), while glossolalia is mentioned several times in the New Testament (Acts 2.1–13; 10.44–46; 19.6; 1 Cor. 12 and 14).

According to the book of Genesis, people originally spoke one language but when they built a tower at Babel to reach the heavens, God decided they were trying to become like him, so he confused them by giving them different languages and they had to abandon the task because of the unexpected communication difficulties (Gen. 11.1–9). In contrast, the book of Acts describes how, at Pentecost, people of different languages could actually understand one another. Called xenoglossia, this was the reverse of what happened at Babel. The disciples recognized what happened at Pentecost as the work of the Holy Spirit empowering them to bring God's kingdom to the world.

Yet, even though it was a practice of the infant Church and St Paul lists speaking in tongues and the ability to interpret them among the nine gifts of the Holy Spirit, by the fifth century the practice had fallen into disuse. From that time, there is only occasional mention of devout Christians uttering unusual languages – until the early Quakers and Shakers in the seventeenth and the Wesleyan or Methodist revival in the eighteenth centuries.

Even so, it wasn't until the beginning of the last century that speaking and praying in tongues – there is no real difference other than that some people pray silently in tongues – re-emerged through the Pentecostal churches and gained widespread popularity through the Charismatic and Pentecostal movements that began in the 1960s.

The key attraction of glossolalia is the reassurance it brings that the Holy Spirit is working through us, which is why it is encouraged among those who have difficulty communicating with God. 'I used to think that prayer was speaking politely to God,' a middle-aged charismatic told me.

> The relationship was dry and distant. It was only after I surrendered to the Spirit and received the gift of tongues that I realized I had been making it difficult for myself. I was so busy thinking about what to say to God that I wasn't allowing the Spirit to speak through me. Now I know God's within me.

A woman who was reluctant to pray in tongues at first explained it this way:

> I felt a fool at first but through tongues I was able to let go of my intellect and align my will with that of the Holy Trinity. It's a privilege, which edifies and builds you up. It honours God. I often pray for others in tongues. I think of them while speaking the words of the Holy Spirit.

She added that, like saying the prayers of the rosary or centring words, she often uttered a few words in tongues while meditating on the gospel or offering God other prayers of confession, praise, thanksgiving and intercession.

Nevertheless, the gift of tongues does have its detractors. Sceptics regard it as gibberish masquerading as prayer, and linguists who've studied glossolalia point to similarities with the language of schizophrenics and those suffering hysteria. In his 1972 book, *The Psychology of Speaking in Tongues*, John P. Kildahl found that although those who practise glossolalia may have suffered more crises in their lives and be more willing to depend on authority figures than most, there was no evidence of this being a sign of mental disorder. Instead, he found lowered levels of stress among those who speak in tongues.

In 2006, neuroscientist Andrew P. Newberg and others in his team at the University of Pennsylvania published a report on their SPEC scans of the brains of five women praying in tongues. The researchers found activity in the brain's centre related to self-control decreased, but increased in the parts of the brain associated with emotion. Newberg concluded that this is because of the 'very intense experience of how the self relates to God' – which is what we would expect to happen if we allow the Holy Spirit to take control of our lives and inspire us.

Other scholars mention how those practising other religions and pagan rites use utterances similar to Christian glossolalia. William T. Samarin, professor of anthropology and linguistics at the University of Toronto, says:

> Glossolalia consists of strings of meaningless syllables made up of sounds taken from those familiar to the speaker and put together more or less haphazardly . . . Glossolalia is language-like because the speaker unconsciously wants it to be language-like. Yet, in spite of superficial similarities, glossolalia fundamentally is not language.
>
> (*Tongues of Men and Angels: The Religious Language of Pentecostalism*, p. 227)

Yet, we don't reason that because others use the English language as we do, then our use of the language is in some way suspect or invalid. Nor is glossolalia invalid because linguistic research shows it is not a language. A linguistic study of the inarticulate loving endearments couples utter might well come to the same conclusion. The language of tongues doesn't have to be a 'proper' language. Your prayerful and seemingly unintelligible utterances could well be from the Holy Spirit.

Learning to pray in tongues isn't a matter of inventing an obscure, secret language in order to give you an advantage when communicating with God. Neither is it imitating the prayerful utterances of those who already have the gift of tongues. The words must flow naturally from the Holy Spirit. That involves opening yourself to the Spirit in total trust and letting the Spirit lead you.

You could begin by praying aloud in your own language. This helps to overcome self-consciousness about praying in tongues. Ask God to grant you this gift, then remain silent, refraining from using any language you've learned. After a time you may find you want to express your feelings to God. Don't just sit back waiting for something to happen. Open your mouth and speak out in confidence that the Lord will give you the words. Many beginners launch into inarticulate babble, by fluttering the tongue or pronouncing the same syllables over and over like children before they learn a language. To get beyond this phase it might be worth avoiding repetitions and letting new syllables flow.

At first, you'll probably feel you're making the words up and will want to deny that they're a gift from God, but continue to trust that through the power of the Holy Spirit he is giving you the words to praise and adore him.

St Paul offers some cautionary advice about using tongues in the Christian community. 'I thank God', he says, 'that I speak in tongues more than all of you. But in the church I would rather speak five intelligible words to instruct others than ten thousand words in a tongue' (1 Cor. 14.18–19). Paul warns that the utterances are usually unintelligible to others and non-believers might think the person speaking in tongues is mad. For this reason, he suggests those who pray in tongues at church meetings should also pray for the power of interpretation (1 Cor. 14.22–40).

Usually the gift of interpreting a prophecy in tongues will come from another Christian, so if you feel that the Holy Spirit is speaking through you to the community, take heed of Paul's advice and listen to those known for their gifts of wisdom, interpretation and discernment. Remember that the Holy Spirit works through others as well as you.

In rare instances, witnesses report tongue-speakers communicating in a recognizable language they've never learned, as happened at Pentecost when the disciples received the Holy Spirit (Acts 2.1–13). Usually, though, the knowledge of the language is limited and is likely to have been acquired through casual contacts with those who speak the language. Seeking xenoglossia or to be able to interpret someone else's glossolalia as an intelligible foreign language is not the aim of praying in tongues, but to allow the Holy Spirit to work in you to help further his kingdom of love and salvation is.

After a few months you might find you're praying in tongues less frequently. If this happens, don't try to force the tongues. The Spirit may be leading you into a period of quiet communication where you rest in the love of the Lord (see 'The mystical way', pp. 150–8) or to communicate in some other way.

8

CONTEMPLATIVE PRAYER

Contemplation

Sometimes, when I'm telling my wife something unimportant, she'll say, 'Shhh, you talk too much. You don't have to say anything. Let's be still and enjoy the moment together.' We have reached a point where it is enough just to be with each other and share feelings of warmth and tenderness in silent communion. Words would break the spell.

This can also happen in our relationship with God. We can feel that he is so close, within and about us, that we no longer need to reach out with words. My wife spent six years as a sister in an Anglican religious order and as well as the daily offices – when she prayed set prayers with the rest of the community – she spent much of her time in silent contemplation, recognizing that she was in God's presence. The psalmist tells us to 'Be still, and know that I am God' (Ps. 46.10). So, why not follow this advice and silently savour your time with him? In theological language, you could transcend the symbols to approach the reality, so that you allow God's love to overwhelm you.

Shut out all thoughts and images and remain quietly in God's presence, absorbing and reflecting his love. The Spanish Carmelite friar, St John of the Cross (1542–91), explains it this way.

> A person likes to remain alone in loving awareness of God, without particular considerations, in interior peace and quiet and repose, and that he prefers to remain only in the general, loving awareness and knowledge without any particular knowledge or understanding . . . The more habituated he becomes to this calm, the deeper his experience of the general, loving knowledge of God will grow.
>
> (*Ascent of Mount Carmel*, II.13)

At first, the experience may last only a few moments but, as St John mentions, it could soon develop into longer periods.

You might find that once you've placed yourself in the presence of God you feel even closer to him. The warm-up procedure, described in 'Making contact' (see pp. 28–9), and the methods described in 'Imagining his presence' (see pp. 25–7) can move us toward contemplation, as they are a way of eliminating distractions and placing ourselves in God's presence. I've frequently used this type of preparation with parish groups as a lead into short five-to-ten-minute periods of contemplation. And, despite some writers who've regarded contemplation as an advanced form of prayer, I've been pleasantly surprised at the positive reactions. Pre-teens and teenagers, as well as adults, have made comments afterwards like, 'What a fabulous way to pray. I never know what to say to God anyway but this time I felt so relaxed and warm in his love.'

Be warned, though, that contemplation is not about having a feel-good warm fuzzies session with God. It's about being still in his presence and allowing his love to challenge and inspire you.

With experience, contemplation will come more easily – not only at scheduled prayer times but also throughout the day. Don't try to force contemplation so that you feel God's presence. Remain trusting, avoiding distractions that could disturb your inner stillness.

If you find your attention meandering, it can help to have a single short word that will enable you to centre again on God. The anonymous fourteenth-century author of *The Cloud of Unknowing* advises: 'A one-syllable word like "God" or "love" is best. But choose one that is meaningful to you. Then fix it in your mind so that it will remain there come what may' (Ch. 7). Return to the centring word whenever you need to refocus on God. If you find you're becoming restless during contemplation and the centring word doesn't help, then try some other form of prayer.

Three Trappist monks, William Meninger, Basil Pennington (1931–2005) and Thomas Keating (1923–) at St Joseph's Abbey in Spencer, Massachusetts, turned centring into a simple method of prayer in the 1970s. They suggest using the following method twice a day for about 20 to 30 minutes:

1 Ask God to help you select a sacred word that symbolizes his intent and action to meet the need within you. Possible words are: God, Jesus, Abba, Father, Mother, Mary, Amen, Love, Peace, Mercy, Listen, Let Go, Silence, Stillness, Faith, Trust.
2 While sitting comfortably with eyes closed, introduce the centring word.
3 Whenever you have thoughts, feelings, images or start to meditate on anything, return gently to the centring word.
4 At the end of the prayer time, remain silent for several minutes.

Centring prayer helps us to learn to be silent in God's presence and to recognize the fruits of our prayer becoming apparent in our lives rather than just during prayer times.

As with most contemplative prayer methods, centring prayer is not a way of creating a unique relationship with God, a relaxation exercise or a gift of God. It is not an intellectual or emotional exercise but is a way of developing faith in God through his presence within us.

You may also prefer to use the Jesus Prayer (or some other Christian mantra) as a vehicle for contemplation. The constant repetition of the words 'Lord Jesus Christ, Son of God, have mercy on me a sinner' acts as a spiritual centrifugal force to draw you back to the divine presence without intruding on interior silence (see 'The Jesus Prayer', pp. 146–50).

Although contemplation is primarily a silent resting in the Lord, there will be occasions when you will be so overwhelmed with his love that you'll long to express these feelings. When two lovers are together, they often declare their love by repeating simple endearments like 'I love you' or 'You mean everything to me.' To an outsider the words might seem like trite and embarrassing sweet nothings, while to the couple they are attempts to express their devotion. You might like to express your love to God in the same way.

Let your adoration spill out in short endearments or aspirations (see 'Cries from the heart', pp. 41–2). St Francis of Assisi exclaimed, 'My God and my all', as his meditation prayer, while St Thérèse de Lisieux (1873–97) phrased her sentiments more passionately: 'O my Jesus, draw me into the fires of your love and unite me so closely to yourself that you may live and act in me.' Last century, Pope John XXIII (1881–1963) cried, 'O my God, may my only reward be – your mercy.' Often you may find that words of love like this will rise spontaneously from the heart throughout the day, not just during your set time of prayer.

As contemplation is a unique, individual experience – an open style of prayer with little structure done in solitude – it can be misconstrued. Sometimes beginners look upon contemplation as an exotic or elite form of prayer and attempt to plunge into it without sufficient preparation or an adequate understanding of what is involved.

Contemplation normally flows out of an appreciation of God through study, meditation, verbal prayer, self-examination, humility and living the faith. Beginners can also become impatient with the extended periods of stillness or have misguided expectations of spectacular revelations when God will speak to them in the 'still small voice of calm'. Rarely, contemplation may indeed lead to visions or hallucinations.

Some people, including a few writers in silent religious orders – who obviously have a stake in contemplative methods – have maintained that the aim of prayer is silent contemplation with God. But even though Jesus told us to pray in private (Matt. 6.6), that doesn't mean our prayers have to be wordless or silent. Jesus taught us to *say* the Lord's Prayer and often prayed aloud, as did the earliest Christians. Contemplation is one approach to God. For these reasons, it is advisable to have spiritual guidance from a trained mentor (see 'The spiritual director', pp. 180–2).

Is contemplation spiritual escapism, retreating into yourself to have a private special relationship with God to the exclusion of the rest of the world? Of course not. If contemplation helps to fill you with God's love, this will surely radiate through you to others and touch their lives.

The Jesus Prayer

'Lord Jesus Christ, Son of God, have mercy on me, a sinner' – much of the gospel message is said to be embodied in this short, ancient prayer that began with the Desert Fathers of the fifth century. Because of its simplicity and brevity, it is easily understood and remembered and can be said at any time and in any place. The Jesus Prayer can be effective during those dry spells when our thoughts begin to wander. It's among the most versatile of all prayers for you can use it as a warm-up, as a close-up meditation, as a one-liner, as centring prayer (see 'Contemplation', pp. 144–5) or as a background mantra for contemplation and the mystical way.

St Simeon (d. 1429), Byzantine theologian, linguist and early fifteenth-century Archbishop of Thessalonica, stresses that these dozen words are among the most significant we can pray:

It is a prayer and a vow and a confession of faith, conferring upon us the Holy Spirit and divine gifts, cleansing the heart, driving out devils. It is the indwelling presence of Jesus Christ within us, and a fountain of spiritual reflections and divine thoughts. It is remission of sins, healing of soul and body, and shining of divine illumination; it is a well of God's mercy, bestowing upon the humble revelations and initiation into the mysteries of God. It is our only salvation, for it contains within itself the saving Name of Our God, the only Name upon which we call, the Name of Jesus Christ the Son of God.

(*The Art of Prayer: An Orthodox Anthology*, pp. 88–9)

The Jesus Prayer has its origins in the Gospels. Bartimaeus appealed to Jesus, 'Jesus, Son of David, have mercy on me!' (Mark 10.47; Luke 18.39). The lepers offered similar entreaties (Luke 17.13) and the tax collector beat his breast and cried, 'God, have mercy on me, a sinner' (Luke 18.13).

Several of the Desert Fathers prayed the name of Jesus, and the phrase 'Lord, have mercy' (*Kyrie eleison*) is a congregational response in the Eucharist that began with the early Church. But the two parts of the Jesus Prayer – the invocation of the various names of Jesus and the acknowledgement of our need for his loving mercy – didn't appear together until the sixth century in the work of Abba Philemon, a hermit priest living in Egypt, about whom we know little. Prayers abbreviate the text to 'Lord Jesus Christ, Son of God, have mercy on us'; 'Lord Jesus Christ, have mercy on me'; 'Lord have mercy'; 'Jesus have mercy'; 'Christ have mercy'; 'Son of God have mercy'; or the early practice of uttering only the name of Jesus.

The table on p. 148 helps us to take a close look at the words of the prayer.

Some criticize the Jesus Prayer for dwelling on our sinfulness rather than the positive aspects of our faith, like hope and joy. Yet, the writer of the First Epistle of St John reminds us, 'If we claim to be without sin, we deceive ourselves and the truth is not in us' (1 John 1.8). That means each of us has to recognize it is only through Christ's sacrifice that we receive God's love and mercy. Our joy and hope come from knowing we are forgiven and loved.

Although people don't usually use the Jesus Prayer as a close-up meditation, you might begin this way to gain an intellectual grasp of its implications before using it in the more traditional manner.

Lord	Here we acknowledge, like doubting Thomas when he first met the risen Christ, that Jesus is our Lord and that God is the master and ruler of our lives (John 20.24–29).
Jesus	The name 'Jesus' literally means 'God saves' and underlines Christ's saving mission. But as it was also a common Jewish name found etched on scores of first-century Judean ossuaries, or bone boxes, it reminds us of how God took ordinary human form and came to dwell among us.
Christ	This is a special title reserved for anointed kings of Israel. The Jews of Jesus' time were awaiting a saviour-king or messiah to overcome Roman rule and maybe a priestly messiah as well. Jesus had a different type of salvation in mind. At his trial he told Pilate, 'My kingdom is not of this world' (John 18.36). The kingdom Christ sought was over our hearts, minds, souls and strength.
Son of God	This title reinforces that Jesus was Mary's first-born son offered to God, like other first-born Jewish sons, as a 'son of God'. It also emphasizes Jesus' unique relationship with God: 'I and the Father are one' (John 10.30). It is through Jesus that we receive God's forgiveness and redemption.
Have mercy	By asking for mercy, we are admitting our dependence on God. His mercy includes love, compassion, kindness and attentiveness to our needs, as well as forgiveness.
On me	This is your private request to God, as each of us needs to ask for and accept his loving mercy. Sometimes the plural 'us' is substituted to bring home that 'all have sinned and fall short of the glory of God' (Rom. 3.23).
A sinner	We need to approach God in humility, taking a realistic view of ourselves and how we offend him.

In Eastern Orthodox practice, the prayer is repeated over and over as a mantra or mantram, a sacred formula recited inaudibly. To those unfamiliar with the prayer, this may seem like unnecessary parroting, an insult to our intelligence and to God. But the constant reiteration serves as a vehicle to draw us into God's presence. Used in this way, the Jesus Prayer is a form of contemplation. It is therefore advisable to seek the guidance of an experienced spiritual director if you propose to say the prayer for extended periods.

The fourteenth-century monks on Mount Athos, or the Hesychasts as they are often called because of their emphasis on the inner spiritual life through the use of the Jesus Prayer, suggested the prayer be said with the head lowered and the gaze directed toward the heart, while synchronizing the words of the prayer to the breathing and the heartbeat.

The unknown nineteenth-century Russian peasant who wrote *The Way of a Pilgrim* provides us with one of the best practical guides. He describes a journey across country while discovering the virtues of the Jesus Prayer from the different people he meets, the use of a prayer rope to keep track of the number of the times he repeats the prayer and studying what early Eastern Hesychasts had to say on the practice of prayer in the *Philokalia*. He gives us this clear outline of the procedure, which you might like to try.

> . . . imagine your heart; direct your eyes as though you were looking at it through your breast, see the heart as vividly as you can, and listen attentively to its rhythmic beat. And when you have become accustomed to this, then begin to say the words of the Prayer, while looking into your heart, to the rhythm of your heartbeat. With the first beat say 'Lord,' with the second 'Jesus,' with the third 'Christ,' with the fourth 'have mercy,' and with the fifth 'on me'. And repeat this frequently . . . The next step, according to the writings of the Fathers, is to direct the flow of the Jesus Prayer in the heart in harmony with your breathing; that is, while inhaling say, 'Lord Jesus Christ,' and while exhaling say, 'have mercy on me'. And repeat this frequently. Practice this as often as possible, gradually increasing the time, and before too long you will experience a kind of pleasant pain in the heart, a warmth, and a sense of burning. Thus with the help of God, you will attain self-activating prayer of the heart.
>
> (*The Way of a Pilgrim*, p. 83)

A warning to avoid visions of any kind in case of deception or becoming diverted follows this advice. Orthodox writers frequently mention the importance of avoiding mental images. Yet this is easier said than done. When I first heard of the Jesus Prayer, I was very dubious about its effectiveness. It seemed to have overtones of a magical incantation. I was finally encouraged to try it during a retreat conducted by the late Anthony (Bloom) of Sourozh, Metropolitan of the Russian Orthodox Church. As I began, 'Lord Jesus Christ, Son of God, have mercy on me, a sinner. Lord Jesus Christ, Son of God, have mercy on me a sinner. Lord Jesus Christ, Son of God . . .' I felt as though I was stuck in a groove. To try to give the whole experience some relevance, I would pick out a word from the prayer and connect it with scenes from the Gospels. 'Christ' brought to mind Jesus' interrogation before the Sanhedrin when the high priest asked, 'Are you the Christ, the Son of the Blessed One?' (Mark 14.61). 'A sinner' got me thinking about the paralytic (Mark 2.5) and others Jesus had forgiven, as well as my own shortcomings.

Every so often, I would remember my instruction on how to use the prayer and analyse what was happening. Then I would wonder if I should be doing this kind of analysis as I felt that I was turning it into an intellectual exercise rather than a vehicle for coming closer to God and his love.

The advice of Bishop Theophan the Recluse (1815–94) kept resurfacing. He had related his own difficulties in dispelling images while practising the Jesus Prayer and found that the way to rise above this was to be conscious of God within.

> This awareness of the eye of God looking down on your inner being must not be accompanied by any visual concept, but must be confined to a simple conviction or feeling. A man in a warm room feels how the warmth envelops and penetrates him. The same must be the effect on our spiritual nature of the all-encompassing presence of God, who is the fire in the room of our being.
>
> (*The Art of Prayer: An Orthodox Anthology*, p. 100)

Eventually, I found the images and the need to analyse and meditate on the words fading into the background as I felt myself drawn closer to the divine. There were no flashing lights or overwhelming feelings of jubilation – only a quiet, peaceful realization of being in the presence of Christ. Even after I left the chapel, for days afterward I still found myself repeating the prayer in time with my breathing and heartbeat, like a pop tune that we continually hear in our heads. Years later, I still repeat the Jesus Prayer, which is a wonderful centring prayer that continues to bring me to an awareness of the love of Christ.

The mystical way

The mystical way of praying is a mystery to many of us. We often think of it in terms of sensational supernatural phenomena, visions or an intriguing ethereal spirituality – beyond our understanding and on the very fringe of mainstream faith. Yet Christian mysticism plays a very significant part in our Christian prayer heritage going back to the time of Jesus. He told those who wanted to follow him to deny themselves and take up their cross (Mark 8.34–35). St Paul also wrote: 'I have been crucified with Christ and I no longer live, but Christ lives in me. The life I live in the body, I live by faith in the Son of God, who loved me and gave himself for me' (Gal. 2.20).

Mystics try to live this out by adopting the Christian practices of self-denial, study, reflection and contemplation so that they can imitate Jesus. Some famous mystics were St Clement of Alexandria (?–216), St Augustine of Hippo (354–430), Hildegard of Bingen (1098–1179), St Francis of Assisi (1181–1226), St John of the Cross (1542–91), St Teresa of Avila (1515–82) and, more recently, St Pio of Pietrelcina or Father Pio (1887–1968), Evelyn Underhill (1875–1941), Thomas Merton (1915–68) and Anthony de Mello (1931–87). All these people, along with numerous others, have been able to cultivate an in-depth relationship with God through the contemplative life, attaining a special state of union with the divine.

Some people like to add poets and artists like William Blake (1757–1827), T. S. Eliot (1888–1965), and former United Nations General Secretary Dag Hammarskjöld (1905–61) to the list of Christian mystics. But, although these people use remarkable metaphors to give insight into the divine, it is questionable whether they show the fruits of union with God in their lives that we would expect of a Christian mystic.

If we can draw any distinction between the mystic and the contemplative, it would be a matter of intensity; the union with God is the mystical experience. It is at this point the mystic has a glimpse of the glory of God. He or she is able to see through the dark glass, or reflection of God that St Paul mentions, more clearly (1 Cor. 13.12). A number of mystics have written about their prayer experiences and to understand something of the paths they have taken, their recommendations for us and their own poetic descriptions of union with God, it is well worth studying some of their works.

One of the most succinct and complete accounts of the contemplative and mystical way that had a great influence on spiritual life in the Middle Ages and is still regarded highly for its practical advice, is written by fourteenth-century English Augustinian monk and mystic Walter Hilton (?–1396) in his *The Scale (or Ladder) of*

Perfection. He divides the development of the contemplative life into three stages. The first is our knowledge of God, which comes through study and meditation. The second stage is mainly one of affection. At the lower level this takes the form of an outpouring of love for all God has done for us. These feelings, he says, are from God and will come and go, as the Lord wills. The higher level of this second stage comes after we have been fully reconciled to God and have attained physical and inner stillness. Once we reach this point, nothing should please us more, Hilton says, than to sit still and continuously praise God and think about our Lord.

> The third sort of prayer is only in the heart without speech, with great rest and quietness both of soul and body . . . so that his affections are turned into spiritual savour and relish, that he is able to pray continually in his heart, and love and praise God without great letting of temptations or of vanities. (*Ladder of Perfection*, I.2.1)

He also adds that centring words such as the name of Jesus, the Lord's Prayer and other traditional prayers and hymns of the Church will increase our affections for God and strengthen us against sin and distractions.

Finally, the contemplative is able to go beyond physical surroundings, thoughts and feelings to combine knowledge of God and affection for him:

> . . . the soul suddenly layeth aside all that was in hand, as praying, speaking, reading or thinking; in the manner above said, and all manner of bodily work, and listeneth thereto fully, hearing and perceiving in rest and in love the sweet sound of this spiritual voice, as it were ravished from the mind of all earthly things, and then in this quiet, Jesus sometimes showeth Himself as an awful master, and sometimes as a reverend Father, and sometimes as a lovely Spouse. And it keepeth a soul in a wonderful reverence, and in a lovely beholding of Him, that the soul liketh well then, and never so well as then; for it feeleth so great security, and so great rest in Jesus, and so much savour of His goodness, that it would ever be so, and never do other work. (*Ladder of Perfection*, II.3.14)

One of the greatest of all spiritual writers and Spanish poets is Carmelite friar St John of the Cross (1542–91). For his attempts to reform his order and for refusing to obey his superiors' orders to relocate, he was imprisoned in a tiny cell and beaten regularly until, after nine months, he managed to escape.

This dark, humiliating experience tested his faith and influenced his writings. Through poems and commentaries, he describes the process of divine union as a journey that we deliberately choose to take through a dark night. In *Ascent of Mount Carmel*, he emphasizes the need to cast aside bodily pleasures and desires, what he calls the 'night of the sense', as well as emptying ourselves of spiritual feelings and thoughts – 'the night of the spirit'. He reminds us of what Jesus said about renouncing ourselves and taking up our cross daily to follow him (Mark 8.34) and tells us we must rely on 'dark faith', knowing not where the journey will lead:

> It must be like to a blind man, leaning upon dark faith, taking it for guide and light, and leaning upon none of the things that he understands, experiences, feels and imagines. For all these are darkness, which will cause him to stray; and faith is above all that he understands and experiences and feels and imagines. And, if he be not blinded as to this, and remain not in total darkness, he attains not to that which is greater – namely, that which is taught by faith.
>
> (*Ascent of Mount Carmel*, II.4.2)

In *Dark Night of the Soul*, St John explains that this darkness is a painful time of apprehension and despair when God is purifying us so that we might be ready for a new life in union with him. In *A Spiritual Canticle of the Soul and the Bridegroom Christ* and *The Living Flame of Love*, he depicts the purified soul illuminated and inflamed with divine love and uses the human image of lovers becoming betrothed and married to illustrate the mystical union that is possible between God and ourselves.

> The spiritual marriage of the soul and the Son of God now remains to be accomplished. This is, beyond all comparison, a far higher state than that of betrothal, because it is a complete transformation into the Beloved; whereby they surrender each to the other the entire possession of themselves in the perfect union of love, wherein the soul becomes divine, and, by participation, God, so far as it is in this life. I believe that no soul ever attains to this state without being confirmed in grace, for the faithfulness of both is confirmed; that of God being confirmed in the soul.
>
> (*A Spiritual Canticle of the Soul and the Bridegroom Christ*, 22.3)

St Teresa of Avila, a Carmelite nun and friend of St John of the Cross, was one of the first to distinguish various degrees of mental prayer and is regarded as giving the most down-to-earth advice on the mystical way. In her autobiography, she draws the analogy between mental prayer and a garden to illustrate the amount of effort we need to put into prayer. The beginner in prayer is like a gardener starting to cultivate barren and weed-filled ground. The Lord, she says, pulls up the weeds and plants good seeds. It is with his help that we must strive to make them grow, taking care to irrigate them with the water he provides.

St Teresa mentions four ways of watering the garden: from a well, by a water wheel, a stream or rain. Beginners in prayer are like those who draw water from the well. This requires the hardest work, as it requires discipline in prayer, repenting of our sins, meditating on the life of Christ and having an earnest desire to serve God. Like the water wheel, which requires less effort, the second degree of prayer occurs when we submit totally to God's will, receiving his joy and peace. The work is minimal when a stream feeds the garden and in this third degree of prayer the activity on our part is our complete occupation with God and rejoicing at being in his presence.

> The pleasure, sweetness, and delight are incomparably greater than in the former state of prayer; and the reason is, that the waters of grace have risen up to the neck of the soul, so that it can neither advance nor retreat – nor does it know how to do so; it seeks only the fruition of exceeding bliss . . . I know of no other words whereby to describe it or to explain it; neither does the soul then know what to do, – for it knows not whether to speak or be silent, whether it should laugh or weep. It is a glorious folly, a heavenly madness, wherein true wisdom is acquired; and to the soul a kind of fruition most full of delight.
>
> (*The Life of St Teresa of Jesus, of the Order of Our Lady of Carmel*, 16.1)

Prayer at this level 'is not felt as labour, but as bliss' (*The Life of St Teresa of Jesus, of the Order of Our Lady of Carmel*, 18.1).

When rain falls, the gardener doesn't need to do any watering. Similarly, in the final degree of prayer, no effort is required on our part. God himself provides the communication by bringing us into union with him. He absorbs our whole being in his majesty to the point where even the expression of joy would be a distraction. St Teresa describes how, through this union, she rises above her body, her soul ascending to heaven in a state of spiritual ecstasy, rapture or flight during which she says she even levitated on occasions.

> ... at other times it was impossible to resist at all: my soul was carried away, and almost always my head with it, – I had no power over it, – and now and then the whole body as well, so that it was lifted up from the ground.
>
> (*The Life of St Teresa of Jesus, of the Order of Our Lady of Carmel*, 20.4)

Most of us are fascinated by supernatural phenomena such as levitation, stigmata (bearing the wounds of the crucified Christ), bilocation (being present in two locations simultaneously), heavenly visions or visitations, and allegedly living solely on the bread and wine of the Communion host, which have been associated with mysticism. But we must be careful not to make them the measure of mystical experience.

On one occasion, a young woman described to me the hours she spent in a trance-like state before a picture of the Virgin Mary. The figure, she said, would sometimes talk to her, telling her that if her friends only had faith, they, too, would share in the vision. The picture dominated her prayer life.

I have also met young people who've justified their use of hallucinogens as a short cut to mystical experiences. They claimed that this heightened their spiritual awareness, yet it seemed to me that they were more interested in enjoying the highs of a drug-induced trip than in worshipping and serving God. Like the Jews St Paul criticized, they were seeking signs (1 Cor. 1.22).

Although we need to be open to God's revealing himself in diverse ways, it's a mistake to think Christian mysticism is a question of special signs and revelations. Most true mystics are embarrassed by such phenomena, since they feel they distract from the primary aim – union with God. St John of the Cross advises that any thoughts, feelings or supernatural manifestations are an obstacle to overcome. 'But the soul must be voided of all such things as can enter its capacity, so that, however many supernatural experiences it may have, it will ever remain as it were detached from them and in darkness' (*Ascent of Mount Carmel*, II.4.2).

Levitation is not mentioned in *The Interior Castle* (or *The Mansions*), St Teresa's final and most highly regarded work. Here she extends the classifications of prayer through the analogy of a castle within us. God dwells at the centre and the many rooms or dwelling places surrounding him represent seven spiritual stages. Entry to the castle is through prayer. The first three dwelling places symbolize what we can do through our own efforts and God's grace. In the first set of rooms are those who are worldly but speak to God from time to time. In the second are those who have begun to practise the art of prayer, while those who persevere in prayer occupy the third suite.

The remaining four dwelling places deal with contemplative states of prayer. When we reach the fourth group of rooms, we begin to look within ourselves to find God: 'I think I never put this matter so clearly before. To seek God within ourselves avails us far more than to look for Him amongst creatures' (*Interior Castle*, IV.3.3). Brief union with God marks the fifth group of rooms in which we become detached from our surroundings and ourselves and are able to rest in God. In the sixth set, God gives us the courage to become betrothed to him as a mystical spouse and leads us into spiritual ecstasy.

> The soul being thus purified, God unites it to Himself in a way known only to Him and the spirit nor does even the latter so understand what happens as to be able to explain it to others afterwards. Yet the mind had not lost the use of its faculties, for this ecstasy does not resemble a swoon or a fit in which nothing either interior or exterior is felt. What I do understand is that the soul has never been more alive to spiritual things nor so full of light and of knowledge of His Majesty as it is now. (*Interior Castle*, VI.4.3–4)

In the seventh suite, which is God's dwelling place, we become one with him in mystical marriage.

Many other Christian mystics who are worth reading include:

- Juliana (Julian) of Norwich (1342–1416), the English anchoress who optimistically maintained that despite sin, plague and evils, Jesus appeared to her in a vision and said, 'It behoved that there should be sin; All shall be well, and all shall be well, and all manner of thing shall be well' (*Revelations of Divine Love*, 13.55).
- The anonymous fourteenth-century contemplative monk who wrote *The Cloud of Unknowing*. He uses the image of a cloud

coming between us and God's love: 'All that thing that thou knowest not, or else that thou hast forgotten, it is dark to thee; for thou seest it not with thy ghostly eye. And for this reason it is not called a cloud of the air, but a cloud of unknowing, that is betwixt thee and thy God' (*Cloud of Unknowing*, 4). He encourages readers to seek God through love rather than rational thought: 'For in the love of Jesus; there shall be thine help. Love is such a power, that it maketh all thing common. Love therefore Jesus; and all thing that He hath, it is thine' (*Cloud of Unknowing*, 4).

- The German Dominican monk and theologian Johannes Eckhart, usually known by his title Meister Eckhart (1260–1328), who was tried for heresy and may have died before a verdict was pronounced. He emphasized how God dwells within our souls and how we can find him there: 'I have a capacity in my soul for taking in God entirely. I am as sure as I live that nothing is so near to me as God. God is nearer to me than I am to myself; my existence depends on the nearness and presence of God' (*Sermons*, II.20–21).

- The French Carmelite monk, Nicholas Herman, now known as Brother Lawrence (*c.* 1610–91), who spent most of his life working in the kitchens and, later in life, mending sandals in a monastery near Paris. In his *The Practice of the Presence of God* he found God in the simple and mundane: 'We ought not to be weary of doing little things for the love of God, who regards not the greatness of the work, but the love with which it is performed' (*The Practice of the Presence of God*, Fourth Conversation).

- The German Augustinian monk and member of the Brothers of the Common Life community in the Netherlands, Thomas Hemerken or Thomas à Kempis (*c.* 1380–1471) as we now know him. His *Imitation of Christ*, which may include material from manuscripts of other members of his community, is one of the most popular of all Christian spiritual guides. It discourages the intellect and encourages devotion to God: 'Shun too great a desire for knowledge, for in it there is much fretting and delusion. Intellectuals like to appear learned and to be called wise. Yet there are many things the knowledge of which does little or no good to the soul, and he who concerns himself about other things than those which lead to salvation is very unwise' (*Imitation of Christ*, 1.2.3). Thomas à Kempis maintained we should overcome worldly desires and make our hearts fit for God through meditation, and letting him speak within us: 'Ah, Lord God, my holy Lover, when You come into my heart, all that is within me will rejoice. You are my glory and the exultation of my heart' (*Imitation of Christ*, 3.5.92). He also explains the importance of the Eucharist as part of this 'Burning love and strong desire to receive Christ' (*Imitation of Christ*, 4.17.254).

By sampling these and the many other writings of the mystics, you will come to have a fuller understanding, not only of mystical prayer, but also of prayer generally. Note, though, that it's strongly recommended that you have a trained spiritual director if you plan to adopt the mystical way yourself.

9

PRAYING WITH OTHERS

Teaching children to pray

'Gentle Jesus, meek and mild, look upon this little child' and 'Now I lay me down to sleep' are prayers that many of us repeated as children before going to sleep. Our parents taught us to pray, as they themselves had learned, by handing down these well-known children's prayers. They became our special prayers and their nightly repetition helped to instil in us the importance of regular prayer.

St Francis Xavier (1506–52), a roommate of St Ignatius in Paris and a Jesuit whose missionary zeal converted large numbers to Christianity, is attributed with this well-known quote: 'Give me the children until they are seven and anyone may have them afterward.' Yet, many Christian parents are diffident about teaching their kids prayers. They fear they might be brainwashing them or that 'thrusting religion down their throats' might put them off Christianity. They also fear that it might teach them things they can't comprehend and will treat like nursery rhymes or superstition. Yet, studies show that caregivers who actively assist their youngsters to have fun faith experiences through study, worship, community involvement and prayer are the most effective at helping them become committed Christians.

Most young children enjoy memorizing prayers, and teaching these by rote is one way we can assist youngsters to begin their prayer life – especially prayers like the Lord's Prayer, which we use in community worship. It's important, though, that we go beyond implanting a set of familiar words to helping young Christians come to understand what these prayers really mean. We can also encourage children to pray in other ways so that they can be flexible in how they approach God and can develop their relationship with him.

This involves taking into account their emotional and intellectual levels. Preschoolers are emotionally dependent on their caregivers and learning to cope with the concrete world about them. Adolescents, on the other hand, are starting to think abstractly and are beginning to stretch their wings preparing to become independent, including questioning their faith. Theological concepts like the Holy Trinity or salvation can be difficult for adults to understand; they will be lost on 6-year-olds.

When I first learned the Lord's Prayer as a child, I could never understand why there was so much fuss about forgiving people their trespasses, since nobody trespassed on our property and it seemed such a trivial crime. It was several years before I came to understand what the word 'trespass' meant in the context of the prayer. (Modern translations of the prayer have replaced 'trespasses' with 'sins'.) As well as the meaning of the words, think of the theological implications of any prayers that you teach. Children can become confused if they learn 'Gentle Jesus, meek and mild', and later find in the Gospels that this same Jesus encouraged his disciples to buy swords (Luke 22.36), took a whip to the moneychangers in the temple (John 2.14–17) and had harsh words for the religious leaders of his time (see, for example, Matt. 23.13–36).

There are plenty of children's prayer books and prayers on the Internet you might find useful. It's important, though, that you also help your children and godchildren, younger brothers and sisters to create simple, concrete prayers of their own, which relate to their experiences. Try to spend time with each child reviewing the day and discussing how to incorporate these events in their prayers. What would they like to thank God for? Did they appreciate their meals, clean clothes, an outing in the park, a TV programme, a story or playing with a friend? What are some of the things they could mention to God about which they are sorry? Were they mean or lazy? Did they lose their tempers, upset somebody or skip their prayers? What special requests do they want to make to God? Do they wish to include other members of the family, a sick friend or other children who are not as fortunate as they are? Help children understand that whatever is going on in their lives can be included in their prayers.

At an early stage, encourage children to pray aloud with you. As the young often become restless and have a limited attention span, schedule short prayer periods or consider praying while walking together. Perhaps the children might want to offer a drawing or some other creative activity to God as part of their prayers. It might also help to have visual material available – photographs of the family and the children's friends, flowers from the garden, a toy, a doll, or even the family pet – as subjects for prayers of thanksgiving and intercession. A good example would be the mealtime grace when you could provide an opportunity for the youngsters to take turns in giving thanks in their own words for the food before them.

Sometimes children will digress during their prayers. Once when I was listening to my niece pray, she began, 'Gentle Jesus . . .' and then stopped. Her eyes flew open and she asked, 'Have you ever met Jesus? Mummy says some people killed him. Why did they do that?' She was obviously thinking about what she was praying, so we discussed the questions for a while before she resumed her prayers. If I felt the questions were irrelevant, I would have told her to wait until later. We need to use our judgement, to be flexible and open to the guidance of the Holy Spirit in helping a child learn about prayer.

As the children become older, you could introduce them to many of the methods described in this book, such as cries, one-liners, media prayer, letters to God, poetry and song and the scrapbook. You could also introduce some of the meditations on concrete themes, such as reflecting on nature, the rosary, the time machine and short periods of contemplation. The youngster's prayer time should be a positive, enjoyable experience and not treated, or perceived, as a chore or punishment.

It's also important that the children realize their prayers are between them and God and that the aim is not to please you. Avoid exploiting the prayer time to pry into their lives or control them. Their relationship with God is private and sacred.

Whatever prayer instruction you give, children will almost certainly learn more from your example than what you say about prayer. In other words, more is caught than taught. If you neglect your own prayer life, don't be surprised when your children drop the habit and treat it as kids' stuff similar to believing in the Tooth Fairy or Santa filling Christmas stockings. Be open with them about your own spiritual life and share with them your own prayer experiences – the joys as well as the difficulties and doubts. Then children and adults can learn from each other and you can all grow in your prayer life together.

Group prayer

If prayer is an intimate relationship between you and God, and Jesus told us to lock ourselves in a room and pray in secret (Matt. 6.6), why should you pray with other Christians?

When we pray together, we're recognizing we're not isolated individuals but members of Christ's family. Jesus emphasized this when he said, 'For where two or three come together in my name, there am I with them' (Matt. 18.20). We can learn from one another while giving and receiving support and encouragement. Many of us find it easier to pray together than alone, since we're making a commitment to the group as well as to God.

Almost all local churches have prayer groups. If you don't already belong to one, find out from your church what is available and see if you can make a trial visit. Many groups have specialized interests such as mission, healing and intercession or the rosary. Others combine prayer with study, while some have special requirements for membership. You might look to places of work as well, since many organizations have their own prayer groups. If nothing suitable is available, consider organizing your own.

Approach those who you think might be interested and decide on a convenient time and place. At your first meeting, you'll need to establish some ground rules. How often will you meet? Do you want to include study in addition to prayer? Should each meeting have a central theme? Would you like to socialize and serve refreshments? Whom else could you invite to the group? Would you prefer to limit the size? Who will perform the administrative duties? Is there to be a definite attendance requirement? How many weeks or months will the group continue and what holiday breaks will it take? What would be the best way of structuring meetings?

There are three basic ways to run a prayer meeting: as a quiet time together, as a leaderless group or as a directed meeting.

A quiet time together will enable everyone in the group to pray or meditate in silence. This is especially suitable for prayers that can't be shared or said aloud, such as contemplative types of prayer, or when people of divergent backgrounds and faith traditions make up the group.

In a leaderless group, members have an equal opportunity to pray at random or according to a particular order, although one person usually signals the beginning and end of the session. It is advisable that whoever is praying use an agreed phrase, such as 'Thanks be to God' or 'Amen' to indicate the end of his or her prayer. In random participation, some might pray several times during the meeting, while others could remain silent.

It's important that members are sensitive to one another. Without this awareness, those who are confident at praying in public or those who want to unload what's on their mind could dominate. On occasion, people will begin to pray at the same time. When this happens, courtesy prevails and one person yields. At other times, there may be periods of extended silence when no one will be praying aloud. Members need to appreciate the value of this silence and not feel compelled to fill the void.

A more ordered leaderless style is domino prayer, since each member adds to the prayers by contributing in turn. This works well when the group is in a circle, as it avoids confusion as to whose turn is next. One person begins to pray and after he or she ends with a signal word or phrase, the member on the right (or left) continues, and so on around the circle. Anyone who does not care to offer a special prayer need only give the concluding signal. Whenever I have introduced domino prayer to those who were reticent about praying in public, nearly everyone has ended up by contributing some kind of prayer and often we have gone around the circle several times.

The majority of the groups have an appointed leader and a specific programme (although sometimes the leadership can revolve among the members). The leader needs to take into account the age, interests and social and educational background of the members in planning a programme. It would be inappropriate to pray for human rights in a country that no one knows anything about or to schedule a five-minute silent meditation for a class of fidgety schoolchildren. I've even been criticized by members of a congregation for providing five-minute periods of silent prayer during services. They haven't known what to do during these times as they are used to prayer times filled with words.

The group leader could select a theme and consider the most effective way of presenting it. Many of the methods suggested in this book can be adapted for group use – letters to God, media prayer, poetry and song, the rosary, the Stations of the Cross, the Seven Last Words and guided meditations using the time machine, the close-up, reflecting on nature and possibly the Salesian and Sulpician methods or contemplation. The leader might take advantage of audio-visual aids such as CDs, DVDs, computer videos and slide shows. I have frequently shown religious paintings and objects from nature as the basis for group meditation. I've also used slides of the hungry, the ill and the dying during prayers of intercession.

Offering prayer requests for the leader to include in his or her prayers for the group is popular with large groups or congregations as it gives individuals the chance to contribute to the prayers where they might otherwise be too shy or not given the opportunity to pray aloud. Usually the prayers are for specific thanksgivings and intercessions: Peter who has a broken leg, thanks for Ethel's successful surgery, Doris and John that their relationship may be strengthened, Ruth who has an important job interview this week, the students of the parish who are about to take exams. Many churches have a box, an email address or some other place for people to post these written prayer requests. This enables those who've made the request to stay anonymous.

When my first wife died, I sent an email to one of my church leaders. He wrote one line back saying how he was sorry to learn of that and his staff would pray for me. I never heard anything else. At the time, I felt that his 'I will pray for you' was a way of saying, 'I can't be bothered with your problems, but I'll do my duty and give you a perfunctory mention to God.' It was as if prayer was being used as an excuse for doing nothing more. Effective prayer leadership entails an active interest and concern for the people the group prays for, including seeking updates.

Leaders need to make certain they're really leading the group in prayer. How often have we been subjected to prayer meetings where those in charge treated us as eavesdroppers on their private devotions, put on a show for our entertainment, transformed the group into a therapy session or turned prayer into a sermon? I remember hearing one television preacher praying,

> Lord, you and I know that your people out there have money to spare. But they're holding back on you, Lord. I know that and you know that, too. Soften their hearts so that they may give of their abundance to your great work.

I didn't reach for my chequebook. This pulpiteer wasn't praying; he was sermonizing.

From time to time, we hear prayers for the success of a political party, a favourite sports team, a particular church activity that you consider a waste of time and resources or a military venture. What can you do if you disagree with these prayers made on your behalf?

Bear in mind they are offered to God and he will answer them in his own way. Mention to God how you disagree and ask for his guidance. Then, if the opportunity arises, consider discussing your perspective with those in the group with whom you disagree.

Whatever style of leadership you adopt, it's advisable to have someone pray at the beginning for the Holy Spirit's guidance, perhaps lead you in the Lord's Prayer and then end in a suitable conclusion like this one of St Paul: 'May the grace of the Lord Jesus Christ, and the love of God, and the fellowship of the Holy Spirit be with you all' (2 Cor. 13.14).

Prayer partners

There's something to be said for the adage, 'The family that prays together stays together.' While prayer is not marital glue, couples who can pray together usually find the experience strengthens their relationship with God and with each other. They can support each other and bring to God common experiences and concerns.

Although a spouse would be an obvious choice, you don't have to be married or limit yourself to one prayer partner. You could consider including your immediate family, another relative, close friend or roommate. What about someone who is homebound, who will feel less isolated spiritually? You need only have a common desire to share in prayer and it could enrich both your lives.

The guidelines for prayer partners are akin to those for prayer groups. You will need to establish guidelines as to when, where, what and how you are going to pray. You also need to decide whether you plan to combine Scripture and study with prayer and whether this will supplement your private devotions or constitute your main prayer time.

You could choose to pray silently together, perhaps while joining hands, as you offer your separate prayers to God. Either decide on a predetermined length of time or agree upon an unobtrusive signal, such as opening your eyes at the end of your prayers, to let your partner know you have finished.

Another possibility is to take turns praying aloud. Remember, it is a partnership, not an opportunity for one of you to dominate. Even if you do pray aloud, you might want to draw the line at sharing your confessions. It could come as a shock if your spouse were to discover during prayer time that you had been fantasizing about his or her best friend. This is not going to bring you closer.

A pen pal can also make a good prayer partner. Many have found one through Christian Internet chat rooms or through taking part in prayer vigils for a particular concern. These exchanges tend to be less of a prayer meeting and more of a discussion of one's spiritual life. But even when separated by geographical distances, the partners have a common prayer bond.

10
COMPANIONS TO PRAYER

Props and customs

Many Christian denominations have their own prayer customs and aids. While some of these practices – such as novenas, prayer watches, votive candles and icons – have merit, others – such as walling up and flagellation – are historical curiosities and that is where they should remain.

Icons

Icons are the sacred pictures of the Eastern Orthodox Church, depicting the life and death of Jesus, his mother, saints or angels, such as the archangel Gabriel.

Christian art, especially of Jesus as a shepherd, go back to the earliest times and can be found in the catacombs of Rome. Icons gained popularity after Christianity became an official religion of the Roman Empire in AD 313. To avoid creating 'graven images', artists, inspired by the Holy Spirit, created flat, two-dimensional stylized symbolic images, which were justified as illustrations of God's incarnation in human form. It is therefore God that the icon venerates in a similar way that a poem or hymn can venerate him.

Sometimes called windows to heaven, icons are pictorial representations of a theological truth and are often venerated in the same way as Holy Scripture. Icons may be painted on metal, cloth and wood, often protected by metal surrounds. Because of their symbolism, there is little room for artistic licence. Nevertheless, many critics regard icons as a form of idolatry, while others treat them as quaint forms of religious art.

If you have access to an icon, or a copy or picture of an icon, you may want to try this technique. Place yourself in the presence of God and then fix your attention on the icon. What does it depict? Jesus and his mother? One of the saints? The beheading of John the Baptist or the transfiguration? After studying the scene, think about its symbolism.

Certain icons, like Our Lady of Perpetual Help, have elaborate symbolism. In this icon, well known to Roman Catholics, the archangels Michael and Gabriel are carrying the instruments of the crucifixion; the Greek letters stand for Mother of God, Jesus Christ and the archangels, while the gold background represents heaven. The infant Jesus is looking away from his mother toward his mission in the world.

This isn't a sentimental 'mother with child' portrait but a visual statement of the incarnation.

After lingering on the symbolic meaning, reflect on its implications for you. Some people feel the message is so clear that the icon 'speaks' to them directly.

Sign of the cross

Since the second century, many Christians have made the sign of the cross before and after their prayers. Originally, this involved drawing the right thumb across the forehead to symbolize the crossbeam on which Jesus died. By the sixth century, the sign of the cross had extended to other parts of the body, which is the practice still used today. You do this by drawing the right hand from the middle of the forehead to the stomach, then from the left shoulder to the right, returning to the centre, while saying, 'In the name of the Father, and of the Son, and of the Holy Spirit. Amen.' In the Eastern Church the cross stroke is from the right to the left. The four points of the cross symbolize how we love God with all our heart, soul, mind and strength, while the cross symbolizes Christ's dying for our sins and that it is through him we are offering our prayers.

The holy hour

The holy hour, a devotion in honour of Jesus' vigil in the Garden of Gethsemane and his request to his disciples to keep watch for one hour (Mark 14.32–40), is an opportunity to adore Christ in the Blessed Sacrament for an hour. Prayers of thanksgiving, praise, and for help in overcoming our own weaknesses and our renewal of faith are common.

The annual 40 hours devotion, observed by Roman Catholic parishes, is a longer form in which the holy sacrament is on view continuously from Maundy Thursday to Easter Sunday. On Maundy Thursday, after the sacrament is taken to the altar of repose, it is customary to spend an hour in prayer in its presence, although it is not essential to pass the entire time before the sacrament.

Novenas

A novena (from the Latin word for nine) is a series of prayers over nine consecutive days on a special theme or intention to the Holy

Spirit, the Sacred Heart of Jesus or a saint. This devotion has its origins in the traditional nine days between the ascension and Pentecost during which the disciples – along with Mary, the mother of Jesus, other women and Jesus' brothers – prayed (Acts 1.14). A novena can be private or said publicly in church. There are booklets and Internet sites that specialize in novenas. Popular novenas include those to St Anthony, St Joseph, St Jude and St Anne, as well as many to the Blessed Virgin.

Votive candles

Lighting a candle as an expression of faith began in the eleventh century. It's a custom of the Roman Catholic, Eastern Orthodox and many Anglican Churches and is associated with Christ, the 'light of the world' (John 8.12). Votive candles often appear in front of a statue or icon of Jesus or his mother. When you light your candle, as well as offering your special prayers, thank God for the light of Christ and pray he may work through you and the Church to spread his light into the world. As the flame will continue long after your prayer, pray that you, too, will continue to shine as a witness.

Angelus

For many Roman Catholics the Angelus prayer is associated with the church bells ringing in early morning, noontime and evening, especially in southern Europe and in parts of the USA, as a signal to pray. The word 'Angelus' comes from the beginning of the Latin text, *Angelus Domini nuntiavit Mariae* – 'The angel of the Lord announced unto Mary'. In its present form it dates from the eighteenth century, although its origins go back to the eleventh-century monastic practice of ringing the bell during the saying of the Hail Marys.

Two or more people normally say the prayer, in the form of versicles and responses centred on the Hail Marys.

> V. The angel of the Lord announced unto Mary,
> R. And she conceived by the Holy Ghost.
> V. Hail Mary, full of grace,
> the Lord is with thee;
> blessed art thou among women,
> and blessed is the fruit of thy womb, Jesus.

R. Holy Mary, Mother of God,
    pray for us sinners,
    now and at the hour of our death. Amen.
V. Behold the handmaid of the Lord;
R. Be it unto me according to thy word.
V. Hail Mary . . .
R. Holy Mary . . .
V. And the word was made flesh,
R. And dwelt among us.
V. Hail Mary . . .
R. Holy Mary . . .
V. Pray for us, O Holy Mother of God,
R. That we may be made worthy of the promises of Christ.

Let us pray: We beseech thee, O Lord, to pour thy grace into our hearts: that, as we have known the incarnation of thy Son Jesus Christ by the message of an angel, so by his cross and passion, we may be brought unto the glory of his resurrection. Through the same Christ our Lord. Amen.

Walling-up

This practice began with hermits who withdrew from the world to lead a solitary life of prayer and penance. They chose to be permanently enclosed or 'walled up' in a parish church. Italian anchoress St Verdiana (1182–1242) spent 34 years in penitential prayer in a tiny cell about three metres by one metre next to the oratory or prayer room at the church of San Antonio at Castel-fiorentino, Tuscany. Her only communication with the outside world was via a small window in the church wall, through which she received a little bread and water and a few vegetables. There's a tradition that later in her life two snakes found their way into her cell, adding to her mortification.

Your local church is not likely to prove very cooperative if you wish to reinstate this medieval custom.

Flagellation

Flagellation and other means of self-imposed mortification, like wearing chain mail and rough hair shirts, came into vogue in medieval times as an extreme form of penance and a sign of true devotion to God.

At various times during the thirteenth and fourteenth centuries, flagellation grew from the monastic practice of penance and mortification into a popular movement where flagellants would move from town to town. Whole communities would flagellate themselves, and membership became a way of cleansing sins. The Church declared the movement heretical.

The thirteenth-century hermit, St Rainerius Inclusus (d. 1237), who lived in a cell adjoining the Osnabruck Cathedral for 22 years, was a typical example of a non-heretical flagellant. He wore chain mail and a hair shirt under his coarse habit and flagellated himself regularly until the blood ran. He believed that his self-torture enabled him to identify with Christ's sufferings: 'As our Lord Jesus Christ suffered in all his limbs for me, so do I wish out of love for him, to suffer in all my members.'

Even today, some people punish themselves before they feel worthy to approach God. We should recognize the joy of the resurrection instead of going to extremes in imitating the agonies of Christ's death. After all, he died that we might live and told us that he had come that we might have life more abundantly (John 10.10).

Fasting

In recent years, fasting has been promoted as a quick way to lose weight, make you feel younger and sexier, rid the body of toxins, regulate the bowels, sharpen the senses and cut grocery bills. There are fasts to create empathy with the poor and hungry, to raise funds for various causes and to make political protests. The suffragettes in England at the beginning of the last century went on prison hunger strikes for women's right to vote, while Mahatma Gandhi (1869–1948) fasted for reasons of self-purification and as a non-violent protest to promote tolerance between violent Hindus and Muslims. He fasted, too, to improve the lot of the untouchable castes in India during the 1930s and 1940s.

The Hebrew Bible records how Moses fasted for 40 days and nights while he was meeting God on the mountain (Exod. 34.28). King David fasted in an attempt to avert God's punishment on the son of his adulterous affair with Bathsheba (2 Sam. 12.15–25). King Jehoshaphat declared a fast to gain a victory over the enemies of Judah (2 Chron. 20.3). The people of Nineveh also fasted to avoid God's punishment (Jonah 3.7) and the prophet Joel advises fasting for the same reason.

The prophet Isaiah questions the motives for fasting (Isa. 58). He says the kind of fast God wants is one where the chains of injustice are broken, the oppressed set free, the hungry fed, the poor housed and the naked clothed. With this in mind, some today will include prayers and meditations on those suffering injustice, oppression and poverty as part of their fast.

The Gospels describe how Jesus, when asked to explain why his own disciples didn't fast in contrast to disciples of the scribes and Pharisees and John, replies by likening himself to a bridegroom – and no one fasts while they are with the bridegroom. 'But the time will come', Jesus warns, 'when the bridegroom will be taken from them, and on that day they will fast' (Mark 2.18–20).

The early Christians took Jesus at his word and, ever since, fasting has been practised as an aid to prayer. We choose to deny ourselves nourishment or the satisfaction of some other desire like sleep, warmth or sex, as a symbol of our love and devotion to God so that we might overcome evil and temptations in our own lives and be drawn closer to him. In a nutshell, we fast to feast on God.

This was discovered by a middle-aged lifelong Christian who took a closer look at the ascetic existence of John the Baptist (Mark 1.6; 2.18–20), Jesus' 40-day fast in the wilderness overcoming temptations from the devil – similar to that of Moses (Matt. 4.2) – and the fasting practices of the apostles (Acts 13.3; 14.23) and decided to give it a try. 'At first I was dubious about fasting,' he explained.

> The New Testament offers little in the way of practical advice and fasting has always struck me as being more akin to hair shirts and masochism than a useful prayer tool. To my surprise, it turned out to be more than a diet. I didn't feel as hungry as I thought I would and it really did facilitate my prayers. I concentrated on how my desires often lead me away from God – the devil within me that I give in to so easily. I agree with Oscar Wilde when he said, 'I can resist everything except temptation.' It helped me realize that. I prayed more frequently and felt closer to God than ever before.

There are four types of fasts: partial, traditional, total and interrupted.

- In a *partial* fast, take only liquid nourishment: juices, milk, broth and water. This is a good way to begin.

- After four or five days, you could try restricting yourself to water for several days. This is the *traditional* water fast.
- A *total* fast means complete abstinence from food and fluids and may not be safe for more than a day. Muslims practise a variation of this fast during the month of Ramadan, when they take nothing to eat or drink from sunrise to sunset.
- In an *interrupted* fast the number of meals is reduced, usually to one a day. You might consider this style of fast during Lent or Advent.

Since a lengthy traditional fast is out of the question for most of us who work full time and have family responsibilities, it might be more realistic to consider fasting one day a week.

If you're going to attempt a fast in any form for more than 24 hours, be sure to take these precautions:

- Check with your doctor first and make certain that any medications you are on will not conflict with the fasting programme. Generally, fasting is not recommended for children, the elderly or anyone suffering from heart disease, cancer, bleeding ulcers, gout, liver or kidney disease, juvenile diabetes or hypoglycaemia. Also avoid fasting if you're pregnant, very thin or have a history of anorexia nervosa.
- Avoid diuretics.
- Drink at least four litres of water daily, preferably mineral water; otherwise take mineral supplements.
- Reduce your physical activities. If you do heavy manual labour or have a job such as an airline pilot where safety is involved, wait for your vacation before attempting a fast.
- The hunger pangs should subside after two or three days. If you're still hungry after four days or have nausea, consult your doctor. These are danger signs.
- It's important that you return to normal eating gradually. Follow your doctor's advice for breaking the fast.

Jesus told us, when we fast, not to look sombre or disfigure ourselves as the hypocrites do. We are not to make it obvious to others as we aren't doing it for them but for our heavenly Father (Matt. 6.16–18). Your fast should not be a morbid affair, but a positive experience undertaken out of love for God. It can deepen your prayer life and your commitment to him.

Keeping in touch

If you want to have more than a casual acquaintance with God, you'll need to develop a dynamic, regular pattern of prayer. You'll have to keep in close touch.

That means having a definite prayer schedule. You might like to plan yours for a week or a month at a time. Try to allot at least 15 to 20 minutes twice a day (see 'Finding the time', pp. 17–19). During these sessions, you could include conversational forms of prayer, reading and meditating on other people's prayers and the shorter forms of meditation – the close-up, time machine, several mysteries of the rosary – or even a brief contemplation, perhaps using the Jesus Prayer. If you plan to meditate on a passage from Scripture or other spiritual literature, allow for additional time for reading. Don't let your books become a substitute for prayer.

As most of us are hard pressed for time during the week, the lengthier Salesian and Sulpician meditations and the Spiritual Exercises or in-depth contemplation might be best kept for a weekend or for special times during the church year like Advent or Lent. The Stations of the Cross and the Seven Last Words are especially suitable for Easter. Periodically, for the sake of variety, you might choose to write a letter to God, update your scrapbook or make an excursion to the countryside, the seaside or a nearby park to reflect on nature.

Try to take time for a yearly retreat so that you can get away from your usual surroundings to take stock of and renew your spiritual life. Weekly or Lenten fasts could also figure in your programme.

It can be worthwhile spending a little time writing out an agenda for your meeting with God. It needn't be long or highly structured – just a few notes so that you are thinking of how you approach God and how you can best use your prayer time.

Remember to begin each prayer session by placing yourself in God's presence and asking for his guidance. Don't forget to allow a period of silence for God to speak to you. Here is a typical example of how I have spent a 20-minute evening prayer time.

1   A warm-up to place myself in the presence of God, followed by a period of silence. When my mind wandered several times, I uttered the Jesus Prayer.

2 Self-examination of what happened during the day, my motives and intentions and confession of sin.

3 Thanksgiving for God's goodness and guidance during the day.

4 Prayer for the people I came into contact with during the day, along with prayers for my family, the Church and Christian mission.

5 A close-up meditation on the beatitude, 'Blessed are the meek, for they will inherit the earth' (Matt. 5.5) and a request to obtain that virtue.

6 Another period of silence.

7 The Lord's Prayer.

There are many possible combinations. But, however varied and interesting a prayer menu you have created, be ready to drop your prepared programme if you feel you're being led in a different direction by the Holy Spirit.

A common mistake of newcomers to prayer is being so fired with enthusiasm initially that they spend hours on their knees, setting a pace which is hard to maintain. Not surprisingly, their fervour soon abates as they suffer 'burnout'. It is preferable to begin with realistic expectations and gradually extend the prayer programme.

Try to set aside a time, perhaps once a month, for review and evaluation of your prayer life. If you have written agendas, save them, along with any comments you have made, and make this the basis of a personal prayer log or journal. After reading through your entries for the month, ask yourself questions like these:

- In what way did God reveal himself to me during prayer?
- Am I allowing time to listen to God?
- Did I skip prayers or rush some prayer times so I could get it over quickly?
- How did my prayers have an impact on my daily life?
- Were they mainly God-centred, self-centred or other-centred?
- Have I been honest with God or is there something I'm trying to hide?
- Have I been offering to God all the gifts he's given me – my abilities, possessions, time and energy?
- Are there people who need my prayers, or have asked for them, that I've left out?
- Have I become more interested in the prayer technique than the encounter with God?

- Do I look forward to my prayer times? If not, what positive steps can I take?
- What difficulties did I encounter? Do I need to pray in a quieter place, use a different prayer method, do more spiritual reading, recognize I'm going through a period that St John of the Cross describes as a 'dark night of the soul', or discuss the problems with a spiritual director?
- Am I self-satisfied and proud of my spiritual prowess?
- Did I carry out the resolutions I made? If not, why not? How can I improve?
- Am I reflecting God's love to others?

Your evaluations can give you practical ideas on how you can improve your prayer life so that you can develop a deep and lasting relationship with God.

The spiritual director

When the disciples wanted to learn how to pray, they asked Jesus to teach them (Luke 11.1). They realized prayer is like any other skill. It helps to have a good teacher. In the same way, we, too, can profit from the guidance of a spiritual director, soul friend or mentor – a devout Christian with whom we can share our spiritual experiences and gain insight and guidance. Such a friend can encourage and extend us, as well as help avoid pitfalls such as expecting instant results, giving up when we go through a dark patch when we have doubts or God seems to have forsaken us, overextending ourselves, going off on tangents or becoming distracted or discouraged.

Some of us treat spiritual direction like marriage counselling: we resort to it when our spiritual lives are on the verge of collapse.

We can view our prayer life as a private affair with God and become so subjectively involved that we are not in the best position to take a dispassionate view of our spiritual development. But, although our communications with God are personal, we need to recognize that we are members of the body of Christ and that the Holy Spirit can work through others who have the gift of teaching and encouragement (Rom. 12.6–8).

Spiritual direction is not a form of psychotherapy or even sacramental confession. You might choose to combine your director and confessor, but be aware that someone competent in one field might not be strong in another.

Since the relationship you will have with your spiritual director is akin to that between an apprentice and a master, you will need to look for someone who leads a devout life, with whom you have empathy and in whom you can trust. He or she needs to be adept at helping to increase spiritual awareness and preferably have experience in the same prayer focus as you – be it contemplation, the Jesus Prayer, Christian yoga or the meditation methods. It's advisable to select someone who's flexible, sensitive and perceptive and who can tailor your prayer programme to suit your needs.

Good spiritual directors rarely advertise their services in *Yellow Pages*. They are usually humble people, which can make them hard to find. Begin by praying that the Holy Spirit will guide you in your search. Then consult other Christians for their advice or check with your local church. There may be a local association or list of qualified spiritual directors available (see 'Further reading'). Major sources of spiritual direction are retreat houses and religious orders – especially the Jesuits, Dominicans and Augustinians – who usually welcome anyone seeking guidance. Don't restrict your sights to your own religious circle or denomination. Remember, too, that many excellent spiritual directors are among the laity. The Anglican mystic, poet and writer, Evelyn Underhill (1875–1941), received direction from a German Catholic layman, Baron Friedrich von Hügel (1852–1925).

Gifted directors usually have full appointment books, so be patient. Once you've located a likely person, set up a preliminary meeting to see if a working relationship is possible. Inquire about the director's approach: does he or she plan out a programme for you and monitor your progress, or is it mostly analysis and discussion of your spiritual experiences? How does the director react to opinions that diverge from his or her own? Conversely, could you accept advice? Is there a free exchange of ideas? Do you feel confident in his or her abilities?

If you feel uneasy, don't be afraid to mention this. It's far better to recognize any incompatibility at this stage than later. Likewise, the director also needs a chance to determine if he or she could help you spiritually. When you've settled on a director, decide on the times you'll meet and try to commit yourself initially for a year.

Unlike other forms of counselling, many spiritual directors do not charge for their services. In these cases, it is appropriate to give a donation to the church or religious order concerned a sum similar to that you would pay a counsellor.

Retreats

All of us could benefit from setting aside some time at least once a year to take stock, refresh ourselves and have an in-depth period with God. For most, this will mean a weekend or a few days during a vacation spent at a retreat centre, a monastery or convent, a camp or even at home. Retreat houses are often in beautiful surroundings to help us unwind and leave our daily cares behind. One I went to in the desert near Palm Springs in California even had a swimming pool and whirlpool.

There are various types of retreats. Before you sign up for one, check out what's involved. Most are for groups and may consist of conferences, discussion periods and time for meditation on assigned readings. There is usually the option of a personal appointment with the retreat conductor, as well as leisure time.

The heart of the retreat is the daily worship services, which may include the Eucharist as well as morning, midday and evening prayer and Compline. Sometimes retreatants maintain silence throughout the retreat, or else during designated periods in order to be alone with God.

Rather than a group retreat, you might consider one that is individually directed. Some retreat centres, especially those run by religious orders, provide for personalized spiritual direction. You are usually welcome to join in the Eucharist and daily offices if your retreat is with a religious order.

The majority of conducted retreats are on themes such as spiritual healing, contemplation, charismatic renewal, journal-writing, Ignatius' Spiritual Exercises or Scripture passages. Groups such as married couples, the newly separated or divorced, missionaries, religious education teachers and lay leaders will have specialized themes. Check to see what is available and inquire if there are any specific conditions. Some retreat centres will admit only men or only women. Others do not welcome families with small children, while others provide for childcare.

Some retreat houses advertise on the Internet. Write or phone ahead for specific information, costs and reservations. Retreat houses gladly accept donations and may make special arrangements for those in genuine financial need.

If you can't get away for an organized retreat, you might consider a day or weekend retreat at home, in a vacation spot or at a local church. Wherever you are, try to avoid interruptions by alerting your family and friends, turning off your computer and TV, and switching your telephones to message mode so that others can leave a message for you to pick up later. Map out a general programme in advance, if possible on a theme, and allow for varied activities as well as breaks for food and relaxation. Have available your Bible and other spiritual reading, along with a prayer book with services of morning and evening prayer. Your programme might look like this:

Morning

- Rise early and say prayers of adoration, thanksgiving and confession. You might prefer to do an extensive self-examination and sacramental confession the day before.
- If there's an early service at a local church, you could include this; otherwise, say the office of morning prayer at home.
- Light breakfast.
- Spiritual reading. Choose material from the Scriptures, the *Imitation of Christ* or the life of a devout person, which will serve as a preparation for your meditation period.
- Spend an hour in meditation using one of the methods described in this book.
- Sit in a chair and listen to music or relax in some other way.
- Light lunch (or fast).

Afternoon

- Try writing a letter or a poem to God, or imagine Jesus' presence while you communicate with him.
- Make your requests to God: think of his creation, the problems of the world, mission and the needs of your church, family and friends as well as your own special needs.
- Spend about half an hour in contemplation.
- Take a walk in the garden or a local park, or relax in another way.
- Light supper.

Evening

- Spiritual reading.
- A short period of contemplation.
- End the day with a general thanksgiving and evening prayer (Evensong, Vespers or Compline).

A more austere form of quiet day is the poustinia, from the Russian word for desert. The idea here is that you spend the day living like a hermit with only tea, coffee or water and bread. Seclude yourself in a bare room away from distractions and intrusions from the outside world, with maybe a crucifix or icon and your Bible as companions as you spend the day in meditation and prayer.

This experience of intense and concentrated prayer can only serve to make you more receptive to God.

11
OBSTACLES TO PRAYER

Obstacles to prayer

Most of us run into difficulties in our prayer life. Like any relationship, there will be ups and downs, times when we wonder whether it's worthwhile or whether God even bothers about us. But don't lose heart. Like the rest of us who pray, many saints who specialized in prayer found that the more they reached out to God, the more he became like an elusive shadow shrinking from sight. Many went through dry periods and felt like giving up. Here's a checklist of the common problems and some suggested remedies you might like to try.

If you don't feel in the right mood to pray

If you wait until you're in the right mood, you might never get around to praying. Try to pray regularly even if you feel you're having an off day. Once you begin, you'll probably feel more positive about communicating with God. If you reach a stage where your motivation is almost nil, try joining a prayer group or praying with a friend.

If you're apprehensive about approaching God

It's natural to feel a certain amount of awe when we approach our Creator and Sustainer – especially when we think about our sins and how we've let God down. But that's no reason to be bashful. We all make mistakes. That's part of our human condition. Accept that God really does love you – whatever your shortcomings, including bad habits and repeated mistakes – and that, through Christ, God will forgive you. If you cannot accept this forgiveness, consider making your confession in the presence of a priest or receiving spiritual counsel from a pastor. If it's a question of a rift with someone, take steps to become reconciled. If that is not possible, pray for the person you've fallen out with.

If you're angry with God

Instead of sulking, let God know how you feel. God can take it. He has a good self-image.

If God seems abstract and nebulous

Perhaps your approach to God is a little too academic. You could be thinking of God on the cosmic scale, rather than of the human being who died out of love for us on the cross. Try responding with love. You could also address your prayers to Jesus while imagining him present, or try a contemplative method by which you might come to have an experience of God within you.

If you suspect God might not be listening to you

Are you really listening to him? Your conversations might seem one way because they are. When friends talk non-stop at us, we usually keep quiet and let them dominate until they're prepared to listen to us. Much the same happens with our relationship with God. You could also be going through a desert-like experience, which may last for some time – giving you the opportunity to adjust your attitudes in readiness for God's response.

If you have doubts about whether God even exists

Remember that St Thomas, the apostle, was a doubter also and Jesus answered his doubts. Bring your doubts before God and seek answers to your questions through spiritual reading, discussion and counsel.

If you don't know what to say to God

You don't have to say much. You could contemplate him in quietness. You could also pray one-liners throughout the day or use a prayer book or a structured meditation like the rosary.

Once you begin to pray, you're easily distracted

You might need to pray in a different place or adopt a different position. Did you go through a warm-up to prepare yourself for prayer? You could offer your distractions to God and leave them with him. If you're distracted during contemplation, try a centring word, the Jesus Prayer or, if you're continually distracted, move to another form of prayer.

If some of the excitement has gone

You can't expect an emotional high every time you pray. Aim to develop a mature, ongoing relationship with God rather than striving for consolations and pleasant feelings or trying desperately to recapture the thrill of the honeymoon period of your prayer relationship.

If you find prayer tedious and boring

Are you allowing God to challenge you or are you merely off-loading prayer requests onto God and expecting him to pull off miracles for you? You might be going through the motions of prayer without opening yourself to the Holy Spirit. Perhaps you need to vary your approach, try a different method or alter your prayer schedule.

If God doesn't seem to answer your requests

Are you expecting instant results or a spectacular miracle? You might also be looking for yes answers most of the time. God often says no. Have you offered yourself to God so that the Holy Spirit can act through you to help answer your requests?

If you're uncertain about his answer

Ask God for clarification and seek the prayerful counsel of other Christians.

If you feel God's imposing on you

You'd be right. God's like that. The more you pray to him, the more he's likely to get you to do for him. After all, that's the point of the first commandment to love God with all your heart, soul, mind and strength (Mark 12.30).

Does it matter which prayer method you use?

Like communication in any relationship, it's a question of finding the best way for you to keep in touch with God. That should be your only criterion. If you're having constant problems in any area of prayer, seek the help of a spiritual director. If in doubt, stay with the methods that give you less trouble.

Appendix
Advice from the New Testament on prayer

But I tell you: Love your enemies and pray for those who persecute you. (Matt. 5.44)

And when you pray, do not be like the hypocrites, for they love to pray standing in the synagogues and on the street corners to be seen by men. I tell you the truth, they have received their reward in full. But when you pray, go into your room, close the door and pray to your Father, who is unseen. Then your Father, who sees what is done in secret, will reward you. (Matt. 6.5–6)

And when you pray, do not keep on babbling like pagans, for they think they will be heard because of their many words. Do not be like them, for your Father knows what you need before you ask him. This, then, is how you should pray:

> 'Our Father in heaven,
> hallowed be your name,
> your kingdom come,
> your will be done
> on earth as it is in heaven.
> Give us today our daily bread.
> Forgive us our debts,
> as we also have forgiven our debtors.
> And lead us not into temptation,
> but deliver us from the evil one.'
> (Matt. 6.7–13)

Ask and it will be given to you; seek and you will find; knock and the door will be opened to you. For everyone who asks receives; he who seeks finds; and to him who knocks, the door will be opened. (Matt. 7.7–8)

Again, I tell you that if two of you on earth agree about anything you ask for, it will be done for you by my Father in heaven. For where two or three come together in my name, there am I with them.

(Matt. 18.19–20)

If you believe, you will receive whatever you ask for in prayer.

(Matt. 21.22)

I tell you the truth, if anyone says to this mountain, 'Go, throw yourself into the sea,' and does not doubt in his heart but believes that what he says will happen, it will be done for him. Therefore I tell you, whatever you ask for in prayer, believe that you have received it, and it will be yours. And when you stand praying, if you hold anything against anyone, forgive him, so that your Father in heaven may forgive you your sins. (Mark 11.23–25)

Watch and pray so that you will not fall into temptation. The spirit is willing, but the body is weak. (Mark 14.38)

Bless those who curse you, pray for those who ill-treat you.

(Luke 6.28)

He said to them, 'When you pray, say:

' "Father,
hallowed be your name,
your kingdom come.
Give us each day our daily bread.
Forgive us our sins,
for we also forgive everyone who sins against us.
And lead us not into temptation." '

(Luke 11.2–4)

Then Jesus told his disciples a parable to show them that they should always pray and not give up. (Luke 18.1)

Two men went up to the temple to pray, one a Pharisee and the other a tax collector. The Pharisee stood up and prayed about himself: 'God, I thank you that I am not like other men – robbers, evildoers, adulterers – or even like this tax collector. I fast twice a week and give a tenth of all I get.' But the tax collector stood at a distance. He would not even look up to heaven, but beat his breast and said, 'God, have mercy on me, a sinner.' I tell you that this man, rather than the other, went home justified before God. For everyone who exalts himself will be humbled, and he who humbles himself will be exalted.

(Luke 18.10–14)

And I will do whatever you ask in my name, so that the Son may bring glory to the Father. (John 14.13)

If you remain in me and my words remain in you, ask whatever you wish, and it will be given you. (John 15.7)

Until now you have not asked for anything in my name. Ask and you will receive, and your joy will be complete. (John 16.24)

In the same way, the Spirit helps us in our weakness. We do not know what we ought to pray for, but the Spirit himself intercedes for us with groans that words cannot express. And he who searches our hearts knows the mind of the Spirit, because the Spirit intercedes for the saints in accordance with God's will. (Rom. 8.26–27)

Be joyful in hope, patient in affliction, faithful in prayer.
(Rom. 12.12)

For anyone who speaks in a tongue does not speak to men but to God. Indeed, no-one understands him; he utters mysteries with his spirit. (1 Cor. 14.2)

So it is with you. Since you are eager to have spiritual gifts, try to excel in gifts that build up the church. For this reason anyone who speaks in a tongue should pray that he may interpret what he says. For if I pray in a tongue, my spirit prays, but my mind is unfruitful.
(1 Cor. 14.12–14)

And pray in the Spirit on all occasions with all kinds of prayers and requests. With this in mind, be alert and always keep on praying for all the saints. (Eph. 6.18)

Do not be anxious about anything, but in everything, by prayer and petition, with thanksgiving, present your requests to God. And the peace of God, which transcends all understanding, will guard your hearts and your minds in Christ Jesus. (Phil. 4.6–7)

Pray continually. (1 Thess. 5.17)

I urge, then, first of all, that requests, prayers, intercession and thanksgiving be made for everyone – for kings and all those in authority, that we may live peaceful and quiet lives in all godliness and holiness. (1 Tim. 2.1–2)

Is any one of you in trouble? He should pray. Is anyone happy? Let him sing songs of praise. Is any one of you sick? He should call the elders of the church to pray over him and anoint him with oil in the name of the Lord. And the prayer offered in faith will make the sick person well; the Lord will raise him up. If he has sinned, he will be forgiven. Therefore confess your sins to each other and pray for each other so that you may be healed. The prayer of a righteous man is powerful and effective. (Jas. 5.13–16)

Dear friends, if our hearts do not condemn us, we have confidence before God and receive from him anything we ask, because we obey his commands and do what pleases him. And this is his command: to believe in the name of his Son, Jesus Christ, and to love one another as he commanded us. (1 John 3.21–23)

Further reading

General

Alphonsus de Liguori, St. *How to Converse Continually and Familiarly with God*. Trans. L. X. Aubin. Boston: St Paul Editions, 1900. St Alphonsus urges us toward greater intimacy with God, sharing with him all our concerns in trust and love as though talking with a dearest friend. He maintains that God will not speak to us unless we first speak to him.

Anonymous. *The Teaching of the Twelve Apostles, Commonly Called the Didache*. Trans. Cyril C. Richardson. Christian Classics Ethereal Library. http://www.ccel.org/ccel/richardson/fathers.viii.i.html.

Ashwin, Angela. *The Book of a Thousand Prayers*. Grand Rapids, Michigan: Zondervan Publishing House, 2002. Prayers for public and private occasions on praise, special occasions, worship, healing, birthdays, weddings, death, quietness, growing old and most other aspects of human life.

Augustine of Hippo, St. *Confessions of St Augustine*. Trans. Edward B. Pusey. Christian Classics Ethereal Library. http://www.ccel.org/ccel/augustine/confess.titlepage.html. St Augustine's autobiography of his spiritual journey.

Basset, Bernard. *Let's Start Praying Again*. Garden City, New York: Image, 1973. A general and partly autobiographical approach emphasizing the joy of prayer.

Benedict of Nursia, St. *The Holy Rule of St Benedict*. Trans. Boniface Verheyen. Catholic Spiritual Direction, 1949. http://www.catholicspiritualdirection.org/rulebenedict.pdf. The rules for monastic spiritual life provided by the sixth-century abbot of Monte Cassino that has influenced monastic and spiritual life ever since.

Bergren, Lisa Tawn. *God Encounters: Experiencing the Power of Creative Prayer*. Colorado Springs, Colorado: WaterBrook Press, 2002. First-person storytelling to inspire prayer, encouraging the use of all five senses and to use physical exercises to clear the head, slow down and relax.

Bloom, Anthony. *Beginning to Pray*. New York: Paulist Press, 1970. In these chapters, originally given as talks to people who had never prayed, Russian Orthodox Metropolitan Anthony Bloom considers the apparent absence of God, his knocking at the door, and going inward through prayer to find God within us.

Bloom, Anthony. *Living Prayer*. Springfield, Illinois: Templegate, 1966. Contains an original interpretation of the Lord's Prayer. Beginning at the end of the prayer and working forward, Bloom traces the ascent of the soul from bondage to freedom.

Boyd, Malcolm. *Are You Running with Me, Jesus?*, 40th anniversary edn. Lanham, Maryland: Cowley Publications, 2006. Informal personal prayers that raise questions of justice and faith.

Bunyan, John. *How to Pray in the Spirit: Thirty-One Devotional Readings on Personal Prayer*. Ed. L. G. Pankurst Jr. Grand Rapids, Michigan: Kregel Publications, 1991. Worthwhile thoughts on prayer gathered from the writings of the author of *The Pilgrim's Progress* who wrote from prison while suffering persecution for his religious views.

Calvin, John. *Of Prayer – A Perpetual Exercise of Faith. The Daily Benefits Derived from it*. Book III, Chapter XX. Trans. Henry Beveridge. Institutes of the Christian Religion. Christian Classics Ethereal Library, 1845. http://www.ccel.org/ccel/calvin/prayer.titlepage.html. Online text of Calvin's main ideas on prayer, including the nature of prayer, rules for praying and his exposition of the Lord's Prayer.

Calvin, John and I. John Hesselink. *On Prayer: Conversation with God*. Louisville, Kentucky: Westminster John Knox Press, 2006. Includes the key thoughts on prayer from John Calvin, the sixteenth-century Protestant theologian and reformer, including his thoughts on the value of prayer, rules for praying correctly, confession and a detailed analysis of the Lord's Prayer.

Carretto, Carlo. *Letters from the Desert*. Anniversary edn. Foreword by Lawrence S. Cunningham. London: Darton, Longman & Todd, 2002. Carretto writes an autobiographical account of prayer and his call to the solitary life as a Little Brother of Jesus in the Sahara Desert.

Catoir, John. *Enjoy the Lord: A Path to Contemplation*. New York: Christophers, 1978. A practical guide to prayer with an interesting chapter on how other Christians have prayed.

Catoir, John. *Uplifting Thoughts for Every Day*. New Jersey: Catholic Book Publishing Company, 2007. Daily meditations on Scripture, with reflection and prayer that concentrate on thankfulness for God's blessings.

Chervin, Ronda. *Prayer and Your Everyday Life*. Liguori, Missouri: Liguori Publications, 1975. This booklet, written with a charismatic emphasis, contains useful prayer exercises.

Coburn, John B. *Prayer and Personal Religion*. Philadelphia: Westminster Press, 1957. This helpful basic book by an Episcopalian bishop deals with prayer groups, spiritual reading and retreats.

Connors, Sharon. *Adventures in Prayer: Praying Your Way to a God You Can Trust*. New York: Bantam Books, 2006. A simple inspirational guide interlaced with personal stories on how to pray, heal broken relationships, learn to forgive, find purpose and expect results from prayer.

Cottrell, Stephen. *Praying Through Life: How to Pray in the Home, at Work and in the Family*. London: Church House Publishing, 2nd rev. edn, 2003. Practical guide to help people pray naturally throughout the day.

Galton, Francis. 'Statistical inquiries into the efficacy of prayer'. *The Fortnightly Review*, No. LXVIII. New Series, 1 August 1872. http://www. abelard.org/galton/galton.htm. One of the first scientific studies into the efficacy of prayer.

Heyer, Robert (ed.). *How do I Pray?* New York: Paulist Press, 1977. Twenty-eight Christians, clergy and laity, give their answers to the question of how to pray.

Jewell, Joe B. *The Elements of Prayer: Learning to Pray in Real Life*. Novato, California: New World Library, 2006. A Methodist minister answers the question of how to pray, maintaining that, like writing, it is something we can all do but may need to struggle at to be authentic. Jewell uses Strunk and White's *The Elements of Style* for American English usage as a model for rules of usage, form, composition, and approach for our own prayers.

Jungmann, Joseph A. *Christian Prayer Through the Centuries*. Trans. John Coyne. New York: Paulist Press, 1978. A fascinating review of prayer habits from apostolic times until the nineteenth century.

Kempis, Thomas à. *The Imitation of Christ*. Christian Classics Ethereal Library. http://www.ccel.org/ccel/kempis/imitation.titlepage.html. Meditations on the life and teachings of Jesus. Written by an Augustinian monk over 500 years ago, this classic is the most popular of all devotional works.

Lawrence, Brother. *The Practice of the Presence of God: The Best Rule of Holy Life*. Christian Classics Ethereal Library. http://www.ccel.org/ccel/lawrence/practice.i.html. The seventeenth-century classic guide from a humble Carmelite brother on how to practise constant prayer in the midst of the hustle and bustle of our daily lives.

Lekeux, Martial. *The Art of Prayer*. Trans. Paul Joseph Oligny. Chicago: Franciscan Herald Press, 1974. A comprehensive traditional manual more suited for religious than laity.

Lewis, C. S. *Letters to Malcolm: Chiefly on Prayer*. San Diego, California: A Harvest Book, Harcourt Inc., 2007. Written weeks before his death, Lewis writes to Malcolm, an imaginary friend, on aspects of prayer, including prayers of praise and request, corporate prayer, the Lord's Prayer and whether to pray for the dead.

Link, Mark. *You: Prayer for Beginners and Those Who Have Forgotten How*. Niles, Illinois: Argus Communications, 1976. A seven-week programme that covers conversational prayer, meditation, contemplation, journal-writing, spiritual reading and 49 guided prayer experiences.

List of Prayers. Wikipedia. http://en.wikipedia.org/wiki/List_of_prayers. Online links to traditional prayers from different faiths, including Jewish, Islamic, Bahá'í, Hindu, general Christian, Roman Catholic, Orthodox and other prayers. Christian prayers include the *Magnificat*, guardian angel prayer, act of contrition, rosary, Jesus Prayer, Akathist Hymn, Lord's Prayer and many others.

Lohmeyer, Ernst. *'Our Father': An Introduction to the Lord's Prayer*. Trans. John Gowden. New York: Harper & Row, 1965. A study of the original texts and historical background of the Lord's Prayer.

Lucas, Jeff. *How Not to Pray: A Fresh Look at Prayer*. Carlisle: Authentic Lifestyle Publishing, 2003. Humorously written to debunk myths about prayer like believing that prayer is only about us and believing that prayer is never about us, that the only good prayers are long prayers that we can't pray anyway, and that God is both far off and reluctant to hear us.

Luther, Martin. *Let Your Sins be Strong*. A Letter from Luther to Melanchthon; Letter no. 99, 1 August 1521. Trans. Erika Bullmann Flores. Project Wittenberg. http://www.ctsfw.edu/etext/luther/letters/01aug1521.asc. An alternative online translation of Luther's famous 'Be a sinner and sin boldly' comment in his letter to his closest friend, Philip Melanchthon.

Luther, Martin. *A Simple Way to Pray*. http://www.holytrinitynewrochelle.org/ASIMPLEWAYTOPRAY.html. Online text of Luther's response to his barber, Peter Beskendorf's, request for help with his prayers. Luther suggests dividing prayer time into instruction, thanksgiving, confession and repentance, and, lastly, requests after meditating on a Bible passage.

McMullen, Michael D. (ed.). *Clouds of Heaven: Learning to Pray with the Early Christians*. London: SPCK, 1996. The prayers of the first Christians, many of whom are unknown while others such as Augustine, Athanasius and Origen were influential leaders.

Merton, Thomas. *Praying the Psalms*. Collegeville, Minnesota: Liturgical Press, 1986. Merton maintains that God has given himself in the psalms like a sacrament to the Church and, in praying the psalms, we are reiterating our knowledge of God and our union with him.

Merton, Thomas. *The Seven Storey Mountain*. London: SPCK; new edn, 1999. Autobiography of Merton's spiritual journey from doubt – and enjoying wine, women and song – to becoming a Trappist monk and one of the most influential and widely read spiritual writers.

Merton, Thomas. *Thoughts in Solitude*. New York: Farrar, Straus & Giroux, 1999. Regarded as Merton's best book on the spiritual life, it emphasizes the importance of inner solitude and prayer as a prerequisite to effective love.

Meyer, Joyce. *The Power of Simple Prayer: How to Talk with God About Everything*. London: Hodder & Stoughton Religious, 2007. Aims to make prayer simple and natural. Examines what prayer is and how to pray and when it is and when it is not right to pray, and identifies 'Thirteen Hindrances to Answered Prayer'.

Nouwen, Henri J. M. *With Open Hands*. Notre Dame, Indiana: Ave Maria Press, 1977. Nouwen emphasizes the need to be open, stripping away all defences and excuses, in order to be fully responsive to God.

Online Christian Prayer Requests and Online Prayer List. Keep and Share. http://www.keepandshare.com/htm/online_christian_prayer_request.php. Online prayer lists, prayer groups and prayer request sites.

Patrick, St. *Confessions of St Patrick*. Christian Classics Ethereal Library. http://www.ccel.org/ccel/patrick/confession.i.html. The autobiographical account of the fifth-century saint of Ireland.

Prayer. CrossSearch.com. http://www.crosssearch.com/Ministry/Prayer/. Lists links to sites devoted to ministry through prayer.

Praying Each Day. http://www.prayingeachday.org/prayersites.html. A major prayer and education resource site by the De La Salle Brothers in the UK.

Pritchard, John. *How to Pray*. London: SPCK, 2002. A guide to how to pray for new Christians or those returning to the faith. It includes praying with the Bible, Ignatian prayer, as well as Benedictine and Franciscan approaches.

Quoist, Michel. *Prayers of Life*. Dublin: Gill & Macmillan, 1965. A classic book of simple prayers based on everyday experiences like a boring lecture or seeing a bald head.

Roman Catholic Prayers. http://www.roman-catholic-prayers.com/. Internet resource for scores of standard Roman Catholic prayers, such as novenas, Glory be, act of contrition, Seven Last Words, rosary, popular prayers and blessings.

Stevenson, Kenneth. *Abba Father: Understanding and Using the Lord's Prayer*. Norwich: Canterbury Press, 2000. What did Jesus' prayer mean then, and what does it mean now? Biblical, historical, theological and pastoral analysis combined to explain the different versions of the prayer; its varying gospel contexts; its public and private use; its summary of the gospel and pattern for Christian living.

Teresa, Mother. *Everything Starts from Prayer: Mother Teresa's Meditations on Spiritual Life for People of All Faiths*. Ed. Anthony Stern. Ashland, Oregon: White Cloud Press, 1998. Simple, poignant prayers that go beyond narcissism and reflect how morality and spirituality go together.

Teresa, Mother. *Mother Teresa: Come Be My Light*. Ed. Brian Kolodiejchuk. New York: Doubleday, 2007. Brings together letters Mother Teresa wrote to her spiritual advisers over six decades, giving insight into her spiritual journey, including how she spent over six decades of desolation.

Tertullian. *Latin Christianity: Its Founder, Tertullian*. Trans. S. Thelwall. Christian Classics Ethereal Library. Part the Third, Ethical 'On Prayer'. http://www.ccel.org/ccel/schaff/anf03.vi.iv.i.html. An early Desert Father, later regarded by some as a heretic, who advocated prayer from the heart and an ascetic lifestyle.

Whiston, Charles F. *Instruction in the Life of Prayer*. Cincinnati: Forward Movement, 1972. A traditional approach to prayer: adoration, self-confession and renewal, petition, daily prayer, acts of devotion and spiritual direction.

World Wide Web Sources on Prayer. http://www.cptryon.org/prayer/ links.html. Links to collections of prayers, praying with Scripture, praying with the saints, prayers in special seasons, prayers for specific situations or occupations, prayer writings and guides, the rosary, images of prayer and prayer requests, provided by the Passionist Missionaries.

Wright, Tom. *The Lord and His Prayer.* Newton, Maryland: Triangle Publishing, 1996. A phrase-by-phrase study of the Lord's Prayer and its background showing how understanding the prayer in its original setting can be the starting point for a renewal of Christian spirituality and prayer.

Yancey, Philip. *Prayer: Does It Make Any Difference?* London: Hodder & Stoughton Religious, 2006. Editor-at-large for *Christianity Today* magazine and very popular international evangelical author on prayer asks: What is prayer? What difference does it make? Why and how should we pray? What about unanswered prayer? How should we understand prayer for physical healing?

Decision-making and healing

American Cancer Society. *Making Treatment Decisions: Faith Healing.* http://www.cancer.org/docroot/ETO/content/ETO_5_3X_Faith_Healing. asp? Last updated, 26 March 2007. One-page summary of recent research into faith healing.

Arterburn, Stephen. *Healing Is a Choice: Ten Decisions that Will Transform Your Life and Ten Lies that Can Prevent You from Making Them.* Nashville, Tennessee: Thomas Nelson, 2007. Healing is seen as a gift from God as well as a function of our own decisions and beliefs. Outlines what the author believes are the right choices, and the myths to reject to find the way to wholeness.

Arthur, Kay and David B. J. Lawson. *How to Make Choices You Won't Regret.* Colorado Springs, Colorado: WaterBrook Press, 2003. How to make difficult choices with reference to the Bible and the Holy Spirit. Includes an analysis of decisions made by biblical figures such as David, Josiah, Eve and Jesus.

Ashwin, Angela. *A Little Book of Healing Prayer.* Grand Rapids, Michigan: Zondervan, new edn, 2002. Ashwin provides prayers that recognize how each of us is bruised, weary, or hurt in some way and that, strong or weak, we stand alongside one another in our common need of God's forgiveness and love.

Chervin, Ronda. *Help in Time of Need: Encouragement, Practical Advice, and Prayers.* Ann Arbor, Michigan: Charis Books, 2002. Ronda Chervin's mother, father, husband and godparents all died; her son took his own life; she lost a breast to cancer; her home was destroyed in an earthquake; and she lost her job. She draws on these difficult experiences to offer counsel, spiritual guidance and prayers to those facing loss.

Häring, Bernard. *Discovering God's Mercy: Confession Helps for Today's Catholic*. Liguori, Missouri: Liguori Publications, 1980. The sacrament of reconciliation or confession is seen as a celebration of God's mercy and a source of peace, healing and liberation. Häring describes the revised rite for individual confession, including an examination of conscience using the Lord's Prayer or the beatitudes, as well as a communal penance service.

Kelsey, Morton T. *Healing and Christianity: A Classic Study*. Minneapolis, Minnesota: Augsburg Fortress Publishers, new edn, 1995. A classic on the history of Christian healing, including chapters on religious healing in the ancient world, the case against Christian healing, the influence of medical and psychological developments and a healing plan for today's Church.

Kenebrew, Keith Tyson. *Decisions, Decisions, Decisions: Seeking God's Will*. iUniverse.com, 2005. How to make Christ-like choices through prayer, Scripture, seeking options and guidance, counting the cost, discerning the will of God, yielding to his will and waiting on God.

Knight, David M. *Confession Can Change Your Life*. Chicago: Claretian Publications, 1977. A re-examination of confession in the light of Vatican II.

Linn, Dennis and Matthew. *Healing Life's Hurts: Healing Memories Through the Five Stages of Forgiveness*. New York: Paulist Press, 1978. A practical guide to letting go past hurts and entering into a healing relationship with Christ. It explores Elisabeth Kübler-Ross' five stages of acceptance of death and dying in light of prayer and religious experience.

MacNutt, Francis. *Healing*. New York: Bantam, 1979. A very popular book that covers physical and emotional healing, including demonic possession, by a leading charismatic.

MacNutt, Francis. *The Healing Reawakening: Reclaiming Our Lost Inheritance*. Grand Rapids, Michigan: Chosen Books, 2006. Discusses why healing the sick and casting out evil spirits nearly disappeared from mainline churches after the collapse of the Roman Empire.

MacNutt, Francis. *The Prayer that Heals: Praying for Healing in the Family*. Notre Dame, Indiana: Ave Maria Press, 2nd rev. edn, 2005. MacNutt advocates prayers for healing over time, the need for forgiveness, the healing of faith, and the need to accept God's healing love within.

Payne, Leanne. *Restoring the Christian Soul: Overcoming Barriers to Completion in Christ Through Healing Prayer*. Grand Rapids, Michigan: Baker Books, 1996, reprint edn. How to overcome the three barriers that keep us from becoming whole: inability to receive God's forgiveness, inability to forgive others and inability to accept ourselves.

Porterfield, Amanda. *Healing in the History of Christianity*. New York: Oxford University Press, 2004. A comprehensive work that looks beyond Jesus and the disciples as miracle workers and exorcists, to healing in early, medieval and modern Christianity, including looking at the impact of modern scientific medicine and technology.

Yancey, Philip. *Where Is God When It Hurts?* Grand Rapids, Michigan: Zondervan, 1997, rev. edn. Popular author describes with case studies how pain is necessary for our survival and what happens when it doesn't function properly. He provides tips on how to handle pain and how God is compassionate and can cure the ills of the soul.

Meditation and reflection

Dubruiel, Michael and Amy Welborn. *Praying the Rosary: With the Joyful, Luminous, Sorrowful, and Glorious Mysteries*. Huntington, Indiana: Our Sunday Visitor, 2005. Based on *Rosarium Virginis Mariae* by Pope John Paul II, it aims to teach about this traditional meditation, to deepen love for Jesus and his mother and to contemplate Christ.

Foster, David. *Reading with God: Lectio Divina*. London and New York: Continuum, 2005. A Benedictine monk gives an easy-to-read guide to the ancient art of holy reading and meditation that is relevant for today.

Francis of Assisi, St. *The Canticle of the Sun*. Trans. Paschal Robinson, 1905. Internet Sacred Text Archive. http://www.sacred-texts.com/chr/wosf/wosf22.htm. The famous canticle written by Francis in 1225 in a hut near the Monastery of San Damiano while he was ill.

Francis of Sales, St. *Introduction to the Devout Life*. Christian Classics Ethereal Library. http://www.ccel.org/ccel/desales/devout_life.titlepage.html. Online version of this very popular meditation classic that includes preparation, considerations, affections and resolutions, a conclusion and spiritual bouquet.

Frost, Bede. *The Art of Mental Prayer*. Milwaukee, Wisconsin: Morehouse, 1931. An extensive survey of historical meditation techniques by an Anglican Benedictine. This popular book has been reprinted several times since 1931.

Gottemoller, Bartholomew. *How to Find Happiness: A Simple Yet Comprehensive Treatment of Christian Prayer*. Huntington, Indiana: Our Sunday Visitor, 1979. A good introduction to mental prayer and contemplation, with a helpful section on using images of God as Creator, Father, Spouse and Life, by a Trappist monk with 45 years' experience.

Guigo II. *The Ladder of Monks and Twelve Meditations*. Trans. with an introduction by Edmund Colledge and James Walsh. Garden City, New York: Image, 1978. Guigo, a twelfth-century French Carthusian monk, outlines four steps to union with God: *lectio*, *meditatio*, *oratio* and *contemplatio*. Reading seeks, meditation perceives, prayer asks for, and contemplation tastes the sweetness of mystical union.

Further reading

Habig, Marion A. *The Franciscan Crown*. Chicago: Franciscan Herald Press, 1976. A history of the Franciscan rosary, or crown, and meditations on the seven joyful mysteries.

Harton, F. P. *The Elements of Spiritual Life: A Study in Ascetical Theology*. Eugene, Oregon: Wipf & Stock, 2004. A reprint of a major work on prayer and spirituality by an Anglican priest.

Hauerwas, Stanley. *Cross-Shattered Christ: Meditations on the Seven Last Words*. Grand Rapids, Michigan: Brazos Press, 2005. Meditations on the seven words at the heart of the gospel that emphasize Christ's humanity as well as how God acts to bring about victory through seeming defeat.

Ignatius of Loyola, St. *The Autobiography of St Ignatius Loyola*. New York: Fordham University Press, 1995. Trans. Joseph F. O'Callaghan; ed. with introduction and notes by O. J. Odlin. Begins in 1521 with Ignatius' injury in the battle of Pamplona, his conversion and then follows the next 17 years until the arrival of Ignatius and his friends in Rome.

Ignatius of Loyola, St. *The Spiritual Exercises of St Ignatius of Loyola*. Trans. Father Elder Mullan. New York: P. J. Kenedy & Sons, 1914. Christian Classics Ethereal Library. http://www.ccel.org/ccel/ignatius/exercises. titlepage.html. Based on Ignatius' own spiritual journey, this classic is intended as a retreat director's manual and is presented in fragmentary note form. It contains sets of prayers, meditations and mental exercises originally designed for a four-week retreat.

John Paul II, Pope. *Rosarium Virginis Mariae*. The Pope explains the history of the rosary and its use by the Church, maintaining it 'has the simplicity of a popular devotion but also the theological depth of a prayer suited to those who feel the need for deeper contemplation'. He proposes five new mysteries of light.

Kelsey, Morton T. *The Other Side of Silence: Meditation for the Twenty-First Century*. Mahwah, New Jersey: Paulist Press, 1997. Kelsey emphasizes the role of imagery in meditation in an approach strongly influenced by the psychology of Carl Jung.

Neuhaus, Richard John. *Death on a Friday Afternoon: Meditations on the Last Words of Jesus from the Cross*. New York: Basic Books, 2001. Focuses on the dark side of human experience and our own experiences at the foot of the cross, with the prospect of light at the end of it.

Newman, John Henry. *Meditation for the Feast of the Holy Rosary, 5 October 1879*. http://www.ewtn.com/library/Prayer/NEWMNROS. HTM. Newspaper report of the 78-year-old Cardinal speaking 'from his heart' to the boys at Oscott College, near Birmingham, England.

Peterson, Eugene H. *Eat This Book: A Conversation in the Art of Spiritual Reading*. Grand Rapids, Michigan: Eerdmans, 2005. Emphasizes the ancient art of *lectio divina*, to read the Scriptures on their own terms, as God's revelation, and to pray and live them.

Renoux, Christian. *The Origin of the Peace Prayer of St Francis.* http://
www.franciscan-archive.org/franciscana/peace.html. A brief history of
the Peace Prayer, which first appeared in La Clochette in 1912.

Rutledge, Fleming. *The Seven Last Words from the Cross.* Grand Rapids,
Michigan: Eerdmans, 2004. Seven contemporary meditations on the Seven
Last Words, originally developed for a Good Friday three-hour service.

Shultz, Thomas. *Rosary for Episcopalians/Anglicans.* Birmingham: Regency
Press, 2003, 2nd edn. Provides both traditional and alternative prayers
for non-Catholics as well as an appendix of biblical citations on the mysteries for meditation.

Tanquerey, Adolphe. *The Spiritual Life: A Treatise on Ascetical and Mystical
Theology.* Trans. Herman Branders. Rockford, Illinois: Tan Books, 2001,
2nd edn. A standard text for seminarians on mental prayer and spirituality.

Tronson, Louis. *Oeuvres Complètes.* Paris: Migne, 1857. Untranslated
treatise on meditation, commonly known as the Sulpician Method, by
the third Superior General of the Seminary of St Sulpice.

Wills, Garry. *The Rosary.* New York: Penguin, 2005. A history of the
rosary, including Tintoretto paintings designed to help readers better
understand the mysteries in relation to Scripture and history.

Asian prayer methods

Boykin, Kim. *Zen for Christians: A Beginner's Guide.* Foreword by Gerald
G. May. San Francisco: Jossey-Bass, 2003, 1st edn. A practical guide
to using Zen methods, rather than adaptations of them, for Christian
meditation.

Daishin Buksbazen, John. *To Forget the Self: An Illustrated Guide to Zen
Meditation.* Los Angeles: Zen Center of Los Angeles, 1977. This basic
introduction to zazen includes exercises to accustom the body to sitting
postures.

de Mello, Anthony. *Sadhana: A Way to God, Christian Exercises in Eastern
Form.* New York: Image, 1984. Forty-seven exercises that draw on
Scripture and Eastern and Western methods to teach awareness of
physical sensations, stillness, healing of hurtful memories, and consciousness of self and the wider world.

Déchanet, J. M. *Christian Yoga.* New York: Harper and Brothers, 1959. One
of the first attempts to combine yoga with Christian prayer. The various
elements merge in a personal approach.

Habito, Ruben L. F. *Living Zen, Loving God.* Somerville, Maryland: Wisdom
Publications, 2004. Parallels are drawn between Christianity and Zen
theology, particularly the Zen teachings of dying to desire and self in order
to reach enlightenment as being similar to the Christian experience of
dying to live a new life in God.

Humphreys, Christmas. *Zen Buddhism.* New York: Macmillan, 1963. An excellent historical background of Zen with a description of its practice.

Iyengar, B. K. S. *Light of Yoga*. Foreword by Yehudi Menuhin. New York: Schocken Books, 1966. A major work on yoga, with over 600 photographs of postures demonstrated by the author.

Johnston, William. *Christian Zen*. New York: Harper & Row, 1979. A groundbreaking book that approaches Zen in the light of Christian mysticism.

Roth, Nancy. *An Invitation to Christian Yoga*. Illustrated by Susan Mangam. New York: Church Publishing Incorporated, 2005. Illustrated hatha yoga positions accompanied by a short biblical text, usually from the psalms, for meditation and prayer.

Ryan, Thomas. *Prayer of Heart and Body: Meditation and Yoga as Christian Spiritual Practice*. Illustrated by Elizabeth Pascal, foreword by Jean Vanier. Mahwah, New Jersey: Paulist Press, 2001. Draws on yoga as well as Christian and Eastern contemplative and mystical traditions. Designed to encourage the body in prayer through yoga positions.

Slade, Herbert. *Exploration into Contemplative Prayer*. New York: Paulist Press, 1975. Fr Slade explains how Patanjali's yoga sutras have been incorporated into the contemplative prayer programme of the Anglican Cowley Fathers.

Suzuki, Daisetz Taitaro. *Zen Buddhism: Selected Writings of D. T. Suzuki*. Ed. William Barrett. Garden City, New York: Doubleday Anchor, 1956. This popular book, which has been reprinted several times, is an introduction to the history and meaning of Zen rather than a practical guide.

Upanishads: Breath of the Eternal. Selected and trans. Swami Prabhavanda and Frederick Manchester. New York: Mentor Books, 1957. Pre-fifth-century BC Hindu scriptures.

Watts, Alan. *The Spirit of Zen: A Way of Life, Work and Art in the Far East*. New York: Grove Press, 1994. This concise popular classic is one of the first books to introduce Zen principles to Western readers. It explains the importance of self-control and the baffling spiritual puzzles known as koans.

Wood, Ernest. *Great Systems of Yoga*. New York: Citadel Press, 1966. A description of seven forms of yoga, as well as Zen, the Buddhist Noble Way and Sufi yoga.

Praying in tongues

Christenson, Larry. *Answering Your Questions About Speaking in Tongues*. Minneapolis, Minnesota: Bethany House, 2004. Classic explanation that discusses speaking in tongues as a sign, as a gift and as a ministry.

Kelsey, Morton T. *Tongue Speaking: The History and Meaning of the Charismatic Experience*. New York: Crossroad, 1981. Historical approach to glossolalia from biblical and apostolic times to the twentieth-century Pentecostal movement. Although not a tongue speaker, Morton is sympathetic to the subject.

Kildahl, John P. *The Psychology of Speaking in Tongues.* New York: Harper & Row, 1972. A study of glossolalia by a psychotherapist.

Laurentin, René. *Catholic Pentecostalism.* Trans. Matthew J. O'Connell. New York: Image, 1978. An objective overview of the Catholic charismatic movement, including speaking in tongues.

Newberg, Andrew B., Nancy A. Wintering, Donna Morgan and Mark R. Waldman. 'The measurement of regional cerebral blood flow during glossolalia: A preliminary SPECT study.' *Psychiatry Research: Neuroimaging,* 148 (2006), 67–71. http://www.pas.rochester.edu/~tim/introframe/tongues.pdf. Groundbreaking research showing the frontal lobes, parietal lobes and left caudate were the areas of the brain most affected during praying in tongues.

Robertson, David. *Walk of the Spirit – the Walk of Power: The Vital Role of Praying in Tongues.* Tulsa, Oklahoma: Dave Robertson Ministries, 1999. Popular book advocating the role of praying in tongues.

Samarin, William J. *Tongues of Men and Angels: The Religious Language of Pentecostalism.* New York: Macmillan, 1972. A linguistic analysis of glossolalia samples.

Walston, Rick. *The Speaking in Tongues Controversy.* Longwood, Florida: Xulon Press, 2003. A Pentecostal pastor re-evaluates glossolalia, arguing that its modern use is often misguided, as it was originally intended for salvation.

Contemplation and the mystical way

Book of Contemplation the Which is Called the Cloud Of Unknowing, in the Which a Soul is Oned With God. Ed. from the British Museum MS. Harl. 674 with an introduction by Evelyn Underhill; 2nd edn. London, John M. Watkins, 1922. Christian Classics Ethereal Library. http://www.ccel.org/ccel/anonymous2/cloud.titlepage.html. Written by an anonymous fourteenth-century English monk and based on the mystical tradition of the fifth-century monk Pseudo-Dionysius the Areopagite. Probably the most influential of all mystical writings, especially in the use of centring prayer.

Butcher, Carmen Acevedo. *Hildegard of Bingen: A Spiritual Reader.* Brewster, Massachusetts: Paraclete Press, 2007. A description of this remarkable twelfth-century German Benedictine abbess and mystic's life, along with samples of her songs, prayers, virtue play, letters, theology and medical advice.

Chantal, St Jane Frances de. *St Chantal on Prayer.* Trans. A. Durand. Boston: St Paul Editions, 1968. A selection from the writings on prayer by St Chantal who, under the guidance of her spiritual director, St Francis de Sales, founded the Order of the Visitation.

Diefenbach, Gabriel. *Common Mystic Prayer.* Boston: St Paul Editions, 1978. Intended as 'a simple statement of the beginnings of mystic prayer', this book also contains a good summary of the spirituality of St John of the Cross.

DiFabio, Elvira G. *Secrets of a Soul: Padre Pio's Letters to His Spiritual Directors*. Ed. Gianluigi Pasquale. Boston, Massachusetts: Pauline Books and Media, 2003. Shows the pain and struggles of the dark night of the soul as well as the faith of Padre Pio, who was canonized in 2002.

Eckhart, Meister. *Meister Eckhart's Sermons*. First time trans. into English by Claud Field. London: H. R. Allenson, 1909? Christian Classics Ethereal Library. http://www.ccel.org/ccel/eckhart/sermons.titlepage. html. Described as the 'father of German thought' and forerunner to the Reformation. Eckhart believed God is in man and can be found within, which many regard as a form of pantheism.

Foucauld, Charles de. *Come Let Us Sing a Song Unknown: Prayers of Charles de Foucauld*. Denville, New Jersey: Dimension, nd. First posthumous edition of the writings of this twentieth-century desert hermit, including a meditation on the Lord's Prayer.

Foucauld, Charles de. *Writings*. Selected with an introduction by Robert Ellsberg. New York: Orbis Books; Modern Spiritual Masters Series, 1999. French soldier, explorer, monk and hermit who lived among Muslims in Algeria. De Foucauld's writings had a strong influence on the Catholic Church and inspired the founding of the Little Brothers and Little Sisters of Jesus. He advocates imitating Christ: 'We cannot possibly love him without imitating him.'

Hilton, Walter. *The Scale (or Ladder) of Perfection*. With an essay on 'The spiritual life of mediaeval England' by J. B. Dalgairns. Christian Classics Ethereal Library. http://www.ccel.org/ccel/hilton/ladder.titlepage.html. This fourteenth-century work includes a concise explanation of the stages to mystical union.

John of the Cross, St. *Ascent of Mount Carmel*. Trans. and ed. with an introduction by E. Allison Peers from the critical edn of P. Silverio De Santa Teresa. Christian Ethereal Classics Library. http://www.ccel.org/ccel/ john_cross/ascent.titlepage.html. Regarded as the most significant of mystical Christian writers.

John of the Cross, St. *Dark Night of the Soul*. Trans. and ed. with an introduction by E. Allison Peers from the critical edn of P. Silverio De Santa Teresa. Christian Ethereal Classics Library. http://www.ccel.org/ccel/ john_cross/dark_night.titlepage.html. Stanzas and explanation of the dark night of the soul and the illumination that comes from union with God.

John of the Cross, St. *A Spiritual Canticle of the Soul and the Bridegroom Christ*. Trans. David Lewis with corrections and an introduction by Benedict Zimmerman, 1909. Christian Ethereal Classics Library. http://www.ccel.org/ccel/john_cross/canticle.titlepage.html. Composed while John of the Cross was in prison and written in the same style as the Song of Songs where the soul's sufferings long for the love of God.

Julian of Norwich. *Revelations of Divine Love*. Christian Classics Ethereal Library. http://www.ccel.org/ccel/julian/revelations.titlepage.html. English anchoress who has become popular reading over recent years. She was an optimist who believed in God's healing love in the midst of the evils of the plague and upheaval.

Keating, Thomas. *Intimacy with God*. New York: Crossroad Publishing Company, 1996. History and advice on contemplative prayer providing practical advice based on nearly three decades of experience of centring prayer, which Keating helped to develop as a prayer method.

Keating, Thomas, M. Basil Pennington and Thomas E. Clark. *Finding Grace at the Center*. Still River, Massachusetts: St Bede Publications, 1978. Consists of four articles on centring prayer and contemplative prayer in the Christian tradition.

Kempis, Thomas à. *The Imitation of Christ*. Milwaukee: Bruce Publishing Co., 1940. Christian Classics Ethereal Library. http://www.ccel.org/ccel/kempis/imitation.titlepage.html. Meditations on the life and teachings of Jesus. Written by an Augustinian monk over 500 years ago, this classic is the most popular of all devotional works.

Lawrence, Brother. *The Practice of the Presence of God: The Best Rule of Holy Life*. London: The Epworth Press, nd. Christian Classics Ethereal Library. http://www.ccel.org/ccel/lawrence/practice.i.html. The seventeenth-century classic guide from a humble Carmelite Brother on how to practise constant prayer in the midst of the hustle and bustle of our daily lives.

Meninger, William. *Loving Search for God: Contemplative Prayer and 'the Cloud of Unknowing'*. New York: Continuum, 1994. Meninger uses *The Cloud of Unknowing* as the springboard into contemplation.

Merton, Thomas. *New Seeds of Contemplation*. New York: New Directions, 1972. The chapters on contemplation, mental prayer and distractions are especially helpful.

Pennington, M. Basil. *Centering Prayer: Renewing an Ancient Christian Prayer Form*. Garden City, New York: Doubleday, 1980. An extensive discussion on centring prayer.

Rolle, Richard. *The Fire of Love or Melody of Love and the Mending of Life or The Rule of Living*. Trans. Richard Misyn from the *Incedium Amoris* and the *De Emendatione Vitae* of Richard Rolle, hermit of Hampole. London: Methuen, 1920, 2nd edn. Christian Classics Ethereal Library. http://www.ccel.org/ccel/rolle/fire.html. This fourteenth-century English hermit, Bible translator and mystic ranks alongside Julian of Norwich, Walter Hilton and the unknown author of *The Cloud of Unknowing* in helping us understand personal communication with God.

Teresa of Avila, St. *The Interior Castle* or *The Mansions*. Trans. from the autograph of St Teresa of Jesus by the Benedictines of Stanbrook. Rev.

with notes and an introduction by Benedict Zimmerman. 3rd edn with additional notes. London: Thomas Baker, 1921. Christian Classics Ethereal Library. http://www.ccel.org/ccel/teresa/castle2.titlepage.html. Her best-known work, which describes the inward steps through stages toward union with God.

Teresa of Avila, St. *The Life of St Teresa of Jesus, of the Order of Our Lady of Carmel.* Trans. David Lewis. 3rd edn with additional notes and an introduction by Benedict Zimmerman, 1904. Christian Classics Ethereal Library. http://www.ccel.org/ccel/teresa/life.titlepage.html. The autobiography of Teresa's life.

Teresa of Avila, St. *The Way of Perfection.* Trans. and ed. E. Allison Peers, from the critical edn of P. Silverio De Santa Teresa. From the Image Books edn, 1964. Christian Classics Ethereal Library. http://www.ccel.org/ccel/teresa/way.titlepage.html. The simplest and most practical of Teresa's writings, encouraging prayer as a way of fulfilling our relationship with God through aesthetic poverty, perfect love and self-mortification. She includes a discussion on the contemplative life, vocal and mental prayer and an analysis of the Lord's Prayer.

Thérèse de Lisieux, St. *Poems of St Teresa, Carmelite of Lisieux, known as The 'Little Flower of Jesus'.* Trans. S. L. Emery. Catholic Spiritual Direction. http://www.catholicspiritualdirection.org/poemstherese.pdf. Canticles to the Divine Spouse of her soul, the Blessed Virgin and for St Mary Magdalene, St Agnes and St Cecilia.

Thibodeaux, Mark E. *Armchair Mystic: Easing into Contemplative Prayer.* Foreword by Mark Link. Cincinnati, Ohio: St Anthony Messenger Press and Franciscan Communications, 2001. Simple introduction to contemplation through the stages of talking at God, talking to God, listening to God and being with God.

Underhill, Evelyn. *Essentials of Mysticism and Other Essays.* London and Toronto: J. M. Dent & Sons Ltd; New York: E. P. Dutton & Co., 1920. Digital Christian Library. http://www.thedcl.org/christia/u/underhil/teom/teom.pdf. General theory and practice of mysticism with application to the lives and writings of mystics from the pagan Plotinus to modern mystics.

Underhill, Evelyn. *Mysticism: A Study in the Nature and Development of Man's Spiritual Consciousness.* New York: Meridian Books, 1960. The survey of mystical writers in the appendix of this monumental work and the extensive bibliography are very useful.

The Jesus Prayer

Anonymous. *The Way of a Pilgrim: The Jesus Prayer Journey Annotated and Explained.* Trans. and ed. Gleb Pokrovsky. Woodstock, Vermont: Skylight Paths Publishing, 2001. Nineteenth-century story of a pilgrim

wandering the Russian countryside learning how to make the Jesus
Prayer the prayer of the heart. This is an abridged version.

The Art of Prayer: An Orthodox Anthology. Compiled by Igumen Chariton
of Valamo, trans. E. Kadloubovsky and E. M. Palmer, ed. with an introduction by Timothy Ware. Boston: Faber & Faber, 1978. A collection of
writings on prayer, with one section devoted to the Jesus Prayer.

Brianchaninov, Ignatius. *On the Prayer of Jesus*. Foreword by Kallistos
Ware. Boston, Massachusetts: New Seeds, 2006, new edn. This classic by
the nineteenth-century Bishop Brianchaninov gives advice on how to use
the Jesus Prayer and how to cope with difficulties so that the prayer becomes
the basis of your life.

Gillete, Lev. *The Jesus Prayer*. Foreword by Kallistos Ware. Crestwood, New
York: St Vladimir's Seminary Press, 1987, rev. edn. Examines the veneration of the Holy Name in Scripture and the development of the Jesus
Prayer in the Eastern Church. There are practical suggestions for how it
can be used today.

Ingelsby, Brice. *Pray Without Ceasing: The Jesus Prayer*. Stockbridge,
Massachusetts: Marian Press, 1965. An introduction to *The Way of a
Pilgrim*, a word-by-word analysis of the Jesus Prayer and a helpful out-
line summary written from a Roman Catholic perspective.

Lossky, Vladimir. *The Mystical Theology of the Eastern Church*. Crestwood,
New York: St Vladimir's Seminary Press, 1996. An explanation of the theology of the Eastern Church and how it makes little distinction between
the mystical, the personal and the theology and dogmas of the Church.

Maloney, George A. *Prayer of the Heart*. Notre Dame, Indiana: Ave Maria
Press, 1981. A guide to contemplation based on the Jesus Prayer, the early
Fathers and the spirituality of the Eastern Church.

The Philokalia: The Complete Text. Compiled by St Nikodimos of the Holy
Mountain and St Makarios of Corinth. Trans. and ed. G. E. H. Palmer,
Philip Sherrard and Kallistos Ware. London and Boston: Faber & Faber,
1984.

Writings from the Philokalia on Prayer of the Heart. Trans. E. Kadloubovsky
and G. E. H. Palmer. Boston: Faber & Faber, 1979. Includes commentaries on the Jesus Prayer by Gregory of Sinai, Simeon the New
Theologian and other Eastern Orthodox writers.

Praying with others

Barna, George. *Transforming Children into Spiritual Champions*. Ventura,
California: Regal Books, 2003. An American-focused Bible and research-
based challenge for churches to get alongside parents of young children
and how they can help parents grow their children's faith.

Costello, Gwen. *Jump Starts for Catechists: Praying with Children*. New
London, Connecticut: Twenty-Third Publications, 2007. Small booklet

giving practical advice on community-building and prayer in the classroom.

Geddes, Joan Bel. *Children Praying: Why and How to Pray with Your Children*. Notre Dame, Indiana: Sorin Books, 1999. A mother and international authority on children shares her insights on why it's important for children to learn to pray. Includes practical suggestions.

Harrington, Donal and Julie Kavanagh. *Prayer for Parish Groups*. Winona, Minnesota: St Mary's Press, 1998. Provides over 100 prayer services for groups.

Hunt, Art. *Praying with the One You Love: A Couple's Guide*. Portland, Oregon: Multnomah Publications, 1996. Describes the advantages of couples praying together, including through crises, differences, for children, revisiting evil and the need to keep a prayer vigil.

Jackson, Neta. *The Yada Yada Prayer Group: Book One*. Nashville, Tennessee: Thomas Nelson, 2007. This is the first novel in the Yada Yada series about a group of women who face many crises and how they pray as a group and respond to each situation.

Lindsey, Jacquelyn (ed.). *Catholic Family Prayer Book*. Huntington, Indiana: Our Sunday Visitor, 2001. A collection of prayers from the Roman Catholic tradition for family, children and parents throughout the day, before the Eucharist and other times throughout the year.

McGuinness, Julia. *Creative Praying in Groups*. London, SPCK, 2005. Includes ways of using visual, music and sound effects, dramatic activities and mini liturgies, craftwork and walks as part of prayer and meditation.

Omartian, Stormie. *The Power of a Praying Parent*. Eugene, Oregon: Harvest House Publishers, 2007. This is one in the popular 'The Power of a Praying . . .' series by the same author. Takes the reader through prayers that can be said for a child through each stage of his or her life.

Osborne, Rick. *Teaching Your Child How to Pray*. Chicago, Illinois: Moody Press, 2000. Explains the importance of teaching children to pray, keeping it simple, fun and part of their normal lives, along with the role of parents as mentors and models and teaching children what to pray.

Rainey, Barbara and Dennis Rainey. *Two Hearts Praying as One*. Portland, Oregon: Multnomah Publications, 2003. From an evangelical perspective, covers why couples should pray together, praying through conflict, for intimacy, romance, for the family, along with questions and tips for praying couples such as how to cope with the doldrums in prayer life and hold on to Christ.

Wangerin Jr, Walter and Ruthanne Wangerin. *A Prayerbook for Husbands and Wives: Partners in Prayer*. Minneapolis, Minnesota: Augsburg Fortress Publishers, 2000. A collection of prayers that can be used by spouses together for most daily occasions like meals, concern over finances, lovemaking, temptations to be unfaithful, aging, times of suffering and prayers for the faith of the other spouse.

Companions to prayer

Angelus Bell. Catholic Encyclopaedia. http://www.newadvent.org/cathen/01487a.htm.

Doherty, Catherine De Hueck. *Poustinia: Encountering God in Silence, Solitude and Prayer*. Combermere, Ontario: Madonna House Publications, 2000, 3rd edn. Introduces the Orthodox style of retreat or poustinia to Western readers.

Edwards, Tilden H. *Spiritual Friend: Reclaiming the Gift of Spiritual Direction*. New York: Paulist Press, 1980. An examination of the tradition of spiritual direction, as well as practical considerations: what to look for in a spiritual director, how to be one and how to prepare those called to the ministry.

Evdokimov, Michael. *Light from the East: Icons in Liturgy and Prayer*. Trans. Robert Smith. Mahwah, New Jersey: Paulist Press, 2004. Full colour icons for the major feasts and other important occasions of the Orthodox year with commentary and prayers for each.

Forty Hours' Devotion. Catholic Encyclopaedia. http://www.newadvent.org/cathen/06151a.htm.

Fournée, Jean. *Praying the Angelus*. Trans. Robert R. Barr. New York: Crossroad, 2000. Explains the development of the *Angelus* and especially Marian prayers and the importance of praying the prayer.

Gawronski, Raymond Thomas. *Closer Walk with Christ: A Personal Ignatian Retreat*. Huntington, Indiana: Our Sunday Visitor, 2003. A simplified Ignatian retreat.

Griffin, Emilie. *Wilderness Time: A Guide for Spiritual Retreat*. San Francisco: Harper, 1997. Practical advice on a personal one-day retreat.

Hickey, Marilyn. *The Power of Prayer and Fasting: 21 Days that Can Change Your Life*. Nashville, Tennessee: Faithwords, 2006. The author, who's a televangelist, mainly discusses reasons for fasting, with a chapter on how to go about a 21-day fast when led by the Spirit to do so.

Kelsey, Morton T. *Adventure Inward: Christian Growth through Personal Journal Writing*. Minneapolis, Minnesota: Augsburg, 1980. A Jungian approach to keeping a spiritual journal.

Leech, Kenneth. *Soul Friend: The Practice of Christian Spirituality*. Introduction by Henri J. M. Nouwen. New York: Harper & Row, 1977. A review of spiritual direction in Eastern and Western traditions, the roles of director, counsellor and therapist, as well as direction and the sacrament of reconciliation.

Lossky, Vladimir and Leonid Ouspensky. *The Meaning of Icons*. Trans. E. Kadloubovsky and G. E. Palmer. Crestwood, New York: St Vladimir's Seminary Press, 1982, 2nd edn. An explanation, with illustrations, of the part icons play in the Eastern Orthodox Church.

Maloney, George A. *Return to Fasting*. Pecos, New Mexico: Dove Publications, 1974. A booklet on fasting in the Bible and the early Church, with helpful suggestions based on personal experience.

Nouwen, Henri J. M. *Spiritual Direction: Wisdom for the Long Walk of Faith*. Ed. Michael J. Christensen and Rebecca Laird. San Francisco: Harper One, 2006. Two of the people this master of spiritual direction mentored bring together Nouwen's ideas and method for encouraging spiritual growth, especially through prayer.

Novena. Catholic Encyclopaedia. http://www.newadvent.org/cathen/11141b.htm.

On the Differences of Western Religious Art and Orthodox Iconography. http://www.traditionaliconography.com/webgalleryart.html.

Roman Catholic Prayers – Novenas. http://www.roman-catholic-prayers.com/novena.html. An explanation of how novenas became popular and a selection of typical novenas.

Roman, Alexander. *The Power of the Sign of the Cross*. Ukrainian Orthodoxy. http://www.unicorne.org/orthodoxy/articles/alex_roman/signofthecross.htm.

Sign of the Cross. Catholic Encyclopaedia. http://www.newadvent.org/fathers/1101.htm.

Simons, George F. *Keeping Your Personal Journal*. New York: Paulist Press, 1978. An introduction to the methods of writing a spiritual journal.

Spiritual Direction. Catholic Encyclopaedia. http://www.newadvent.org/cathen/05024a.htm.

Spiritual Directors International. http://www.sdiworld.org/. Website providing information and resources on spiritual direction, including help in finding a spiritual director.

Stutzman, Rose Mary (ed.). *Soul Care: How to Plan and Guide Inspirational Retreats*. Chicago: Herald Press, 2003. Experience and advice from a number of spiritual directors on leadership, prayer – designed for couples, families, teenagers, small groups, individual solitude and special occasions.

Veneration of Images. Catholic Encyclopaedia. http://www.newadvent.org/cathen/07664a.htm.

Wedge, Florence. *How to Spend One Hour with God*. Pulaski, Wisconsin: Franciscan Publishers, 1980. The author suggests dividing the holy hour into 12 segments of about five minutes each: praise, repentance, aspirations, surrender to God, Scripture, reflection, silence, petition, intercession, resolution, contemplation of God within and thanksgiving.

Whitney, Donald S. *Spiritual Disciplines for the Christian Life*. Colorado Springs, Colorado: NavPress, 1997. Disciplines from the New Testament, early Church Fathers and the Puritans, including Bible reading, prayer and meditation, worship, evangelism, stewardship, fasting, silence and solitude, and journal-writing.